Lost to the World

Lost to the World

Tom Adler

with Anika Scott

Copyright © 2002 by Tom Adler.

Cover art by Judith Arnone

Library of Congress Number:		2002096143
ISBN:	Hardcover	1-4010-8388-9
	Softcover	1-4010-8387-0

Photographs of Gustav Mahler courtesy of the Mahler-Rosé Collection; The Gustav Mahler-Alfred Rosé Room at the University of Western Ontario. Photographs of Austrian Border Guards, Hitler Speaks to Austria, Erich Schenk and Egon Wellesz with permission of VOTAVAFOTO Vienna.

This book was printed in the United States of America.

To order additional copies of this book, contact:

Xlibris Corporation
1-888-795-4274
www.Xlibris.com
Orders@Xlibris.com
16817

Contents

ACKNOWLEDGEMENTS

*   *   *

When I started this journey, I had no idea that the path would be so long and convoluted. Fortunately, I had the assistance of many people without whom the facts contained in this book would never have been discovered and understood.

In Vienna, I am greatly indebted to the many researchers who guided me through the thicket of places where information could be found. In particular, historian Dr. Brigitte Hamann, who provided advice and information and also helped locate documents. A very special thanks to Ms. Ruth Pleyer of the Holocaust Victims Information and Support Center in Vienna who was in the case from the very beginning, researching archives in Vienna. She provided me with an extensive summary of documents in the Austrian archives and provided leads as to what further research was needed.

Dr. Rita Steblin, a Beethoven scholar in Vienna, helped in my fruitless quest for a Beethoven death mask which was also missing from my grandfather's estate. My hat is off to Marianne Enigl of *Profil* magazine in Vienna who wrote several balanced and fair articles about the discovery and history of the Mahler manuscript and thus brought the issue out of the darkness where it had for so long resided.

In the United States, Alfons Heck, ironically a former member of the Hitler Youth but very sympathetic to my cause, provided translation and thoughtful perspective to the numerous documents which had to be translated. Dr. Pamela Potter at the University of Wisconsin assisted in locating documents in Berlin. My attorney in Vienna, Alfred Noll, deserves thanks for his diligence and intelligence in pursuing this case in my behalf and for putting up with my endless e-mails. Also, during my travels on the internet, I met Janet Wasserman, an independent researcher, lawyer and music reviewer from New York, who selflessly gave of her time in researching archives. In the process, she became a family friend.

Several researchers in different locations assisted in archival searches: Jürgen Klecker in the Berlin archives, Roger Nixon in the archives in London and Adalbert Kowal at the university in Innsbruck.

I owe an enormous debt to Professor Ed Reilly. Without his herculean effort in indexing my grandfather's library at the University of Georgia and in authoring *Guido Adler and Gustav Mahler: Record of a Friendship,* it would have been difficult, if not impossible, for me to have gathered the information needed for this book. In addition, he, too, has been the victim of my endless inquiries and has given most graciously of his time by reviewing and suggesting changes in the final draft of this manuscript. Also, thanks to Marianna Lee whose sharp editorial eye, sense of style and advice were most helpful.

To my co-author in Germany, Anika Scott, a special thanks for persevering through the many rewrites and for adding her keen journalistic skills, knowledge of the German language, organizational abilities and historical perspective. She and Jürgen Klecker started this journey as interpreters with their excellent ability to look through the nuances of the German language, and it was Anika who first became interested in putting this story in its present form. Somewhere during the writing, they became man and wife, thus adding a happy note to an otherwise tedious process.

And, lest I forget, my wife Louise who not only cares for me, which can be a full-time occupation, but also lent her intelligent observations to this ever-evolving manuscript.

Tom Adler

To all those who weren't as fortunate

FOREWORD

*　　*　　*

B ooks are written for a variety of reasons. The burning
need for self-expression . . . or in some cases self-
aggrandizement . . . money, of course, or perhaps intellectual
curiosity. Some authors find joy in fomenting scandal. Others
are simply unable to engage in personal social discourse. And
then there is the old saw: a desire to leave a lasting footprint
on the earth's surface. The list is long. Although the end result
of this book may satisfy one or all of the above, it was not written
for any of these reasons. My belief is that it was genetically
compelled. I had no choice. Genetic compulsion is best
described as the need to keep doing the same activity that
hounded one of your parents even though it may prove self-
destructive. It is caused by a mutant familial gene much like
any other disease.

I inherited mine from my father Achim Adler who spent
many years and a great deal of effort attempting to secure his
own father's library from a post-war Vienna that denied its
collaboration with the Nazis. Guido Adler's library contained
thousands of books, autographs and manuscripts by many

famous composers. It represented my grandfather's life work. In some strange way, recovering the library was my father's way of ensuring Guido's immortality. In the process, he had little time for me and thus remains a mysterious and distant person in my memory. Intent, as are most people, on not repeating the mistakes of my parents, I set out, in my own life, to live in the here and now. In the main, I succeeded—until what I refer to as the "Mahler Incident" occurred.

Through a bizarre set of circumstances, I discovered that a manuscript given by Gustav Mahler to my grandfather in 1905 had suddenly appeared in a Viennese auction house after being missing for 95 years. When I learned that it was in the possession of the son of a Nazi lawyer who had acquired it during the war, my dormant gene kicked into action: I was compelled to continue the work of resurrecting Guido. There were lots of other things I would rather have been doing, but sometimes one has to play the cards as they are dealt (especially when a runaway gene has been set in motion).

I was also driven by the knowledge that my father had died never knowing about the existence of the Mahler manuscript or how his sister Melanie had been killed in a concentration camp because of her efforts to preserve it. Somehow, each generation has either to divorce its ancestors or to pay them tribute. My destiny has been to try to correct the past wrongs which are set forth in these pages. Forty years after my father's death, I find myself compelled to continue the quest to keep Guido's memory alive and to tell what I know. Perhaps, it will do some good.

Chapter One

SYNCHRONICITY

Sometimes, things occur in such a way that inaction would be intolerable. A fact, an event, a piece of information, presents itself to you in a manner so compelling that some inner voice commands that you act. To find out what really happened, to look behind what has been presented . . . to find the truth.

I was in Paris when I received the e-mail that started it all. After the owner of our Left Bank hotel had given me directions, I wandered through a confusing maze of small tree-lined streets to an Internet café. With my non-existent French, I somehow made it known that it was, indeed, decaf coffee that I was ordering. After a disapproving look, the waiter brewed the offending drink and I sat down and logged on. An e-mail awaited me from a stranger, Dr. Brigitte Hamann. I later learned that she was a noted Austrian historian and author of the book *Hitler's Vienna*.

Dr. Hamann was doing research for a book about the life of Winifred Wagner, daughter-in-law of the famous German composer Richard Wagner and close friend of Adolf Hitler. She had found my name on an Internet genealogy website and knew of my aunt, Melanie Adler. In the Wagner archives in Bayreuth, Germany, Dr. Hamann had found a letter, written in Vienna in 1941, from Melanie to Winifred Wagner. Melanie had sought Winifred's help in preserving the library of Guido Adler, Melanie's father and my paternal grandfather. He had been a famous musicologist and professor at the University of Vienna, and had collected a library consisting of thousands of books and music manuscripts in the course of his career. The letter Dr. Hamann sent to me was the first I knew of Melanie's attempts to preserve the library during World War II. My aunt sounded desperate:

And now I come to the part of my writing that is the most difficult for me, because I want to ask something for myself and because my entire future depends on the fulfillment of my request. And that is the obtaining of a letter of protection that would finally secure some peace for me, my possessions and my work.

From what did my Aunt Melanie need protection? For a Jewish family in Vienna in 1941, the answer was clear: from the Nazis. By chance, I had recently started to piece together my family's history, but what had happened to my grandfather and his daughter during the war had been largely a mystery to me.

I was only an infant when my father, mother, sister and I immigrated to the United States after the Germans entered Austria in 1938. There were few alternatives for Jewish families. My grandfather Guido, at age 83, had decided to stay in Vienna. Melanie remained with him. My father, Hubert Joachim Adler, known as "Achim," was a medical doctor beloved by his patients and friends for his humor and down-to-earth manner. He could speak Latin and several other languages, but not the English he would need in the U.S. My mother Marianne, fourteen years younger than my father, was quite beautiful, and an accomplished pianist.

Though I had never known my grandfather, I could see as I grew up that he had been and remained a powerful presence in my father's life. My father admired and loved Guido, but he suffered from strong feelings of dissociation and guilt for leaving his elderly father in Nazi Vienna, when Jews were being evicted from their homes, humiliated in the streets and thrown into camps.

After the war, my father spent a great deal of time keeping the memory of Guido Adler alive. He recovered a portion of Guido's library that had not been looted during the war and sold it to the University of Georgia. He also made lists of Guido's accomplishments, wrote down what his father had thought about different topics, made family histories and even visited libraries while on vacation looking for obituaries and journal or newspaper articles that may have mentioned Guido. As a child, I resented that my father spent more time preserving the memory of Guido than on building memories with me. Only as an adult did I guess that my father's emotional distance might have arisen out of the hardships he faced when he emigrated from Austria without his beloved father.

I eventually became an attorney and practiced civil rights litigation with a specialty in police abuse cases. In retrospect, this was surely prompted by an intuitive need to right the wrongs that had caused my family to flee from Vienna. Although I had some knowledge of my family's history, I was busily engaged making my own history until I retired in 1997. Only then did I have the leisure to look through family papers in an effort to understand my roots.

All I knew at first was that my grandfather had died of natural causes in 1941 and that my Aunt Melanie had been killed in a concentration camp. Except for my mother's sister Lisl, the rest of my family, including my maternal grandmother, had stayed in Vienna and had also been killed. By the time I started my own search into family history, both of my parents had died and my Aunt Lisl was reluctant to talk about what she knew. There was no one to tell me the story.

Although I couldn't help Dr. Hamann with information on Winifred Wagner, the urgency of my Aunt Melanie's letter strengthened my resolve to discover what really happened to her during the war. I had no idea that this path would lead me through letters, books, family records and archives in Georgia, Vienna, Berlin, Munich, Innsbruck and London. I would discover how my grandfather's possessions were looted by his former students, professional colleagues and a Nazi lawyer, and how my aunt died trying to preserve his library.

The part of Guido's library that my father had sold to the University of Georgia contained a large number of family records, books and correspondence with famous composers and others my grandfather had known. My family history quest had started there several years ago when I had copies made of family photographs and correspondence. I also obtained a copy of a 250-page inventory of every document and book in the collection, painstakingly prepared by the eminent musicologist Edward Reilly. It was by digging into the Viennese probate records of my grandfather that I first found a name that would turn out to be more important than I imagined: Richard Heiserer. He was an attorney who had represented my Aunt Melanie as she worked to gain her inheritance after the death of my grandfather, and his name would appear again and again as I found more letters and documents from that time period.

I soon researched the family records enough to piece together an outline of my own history. In the process, I discovered that there were many items from my grandfather's house missing and unaccounted for. This was, of course, not at all unusual given the actions of the Third Reich. Yet, as I saw the list for the first time in black and white, it made what had happened during the war more of a reality in my life, or, as the saying goes, it "brought it home." Although I was retired, these discoveries awakened the competitive litigator in me once again. Missing were family oil paintings and other artistic works, a death mask of Beethoven, an original Beethoven manuscript and three letters to Beethoven from his teacher Johann Georg Albrechtsberger. Where were they?

When my wife and I returned from Paris in late April of 2000, I wrote a short history of what I knew at that time about Guido and Melanie. I listed all of the items which I knew were missing. To make sure it was accurate, I sent the history to Dr. Reilly.

He and I spoke about it by phone sometime in July. Just before we said goodbye he added, "By the way, have you ever run across anything about the Mahler manuscript?" I was embarrassed to admit that I had no idea what he was referring to. I hadn't focused on my grandfather's friendship with the famous composer Gustav Mahler because Mahler was only one of many noted musicians, directors and composers my grandfather had befriended over the years. I was more interested in the story of my family. Reilly told me that he had found a reference to one of Mahler's musical masterpieces, the song "*Ich bin der Welt abhanden gekommen*" (I Am Lost to the World), hidden deep in my grandfather's notes at the library in Georgia. He had mentioned the manuscript in his book *Gustav Mahler and Guido Adler—Records of a Friendship*. As soon as we said goodbye, I leafed through the book and there it was:

Adler's fiftieth birthday, 1 November 1905, marked an occasion on which, more concretely than on any other, Mahler gave direct expression to his reciprocal feeling for his friend. "With embrace, kiss and the dedication 'To my dear friend Guido Adler (who will never be lost to me) as a memento of his fiftieth birthday.'" He presented Adler with the autograph[ed] score of one of his greatest songs, "Ich bin der Welt abhanden gekommen."

The footnote for this paragraph intrigued me:

Efforts to trace this manuscript have thus far proved fruitless . . . The autograph[ed] full score . . . has not yet been located.

Little did I know that after 95 years, the manuscript would become the missing link between me and the history of my family in wartime Vienna. My search for what happened to it would reveal a story of betrayal and greed that led to the death of my Aunt Melanie. So I added the Mahler manuscript to the list of missing items in the brief history I had written, and decided to go to Vienna to see if I could find out anything more. We planned to visit Vienna the week of October 9, 2000. In preparation for the trip, I e-mailed Dr. Hamann and asked her if she knew of anyone who could help me. She suggested several people, including the Director of the Music Section of the National Library in Vienna, Dr. Gunther Brosche.

On August 28, a little more than a month before we were to leave for Vienna, I sent Dr. Brosche an e-mail introducing myself as the grandson of Guido Adler and asking him if he would have time to meet with me in Vienna. I included the history I had compiled and asked if he could help me locate any of the things missing from my grandfather's estate. On September 4th I received a reply:

I read with greatest interest and also personal dismay your text Guido and Melanie Adler—The Last Years. Guido Adler as the founder of the musicology faculty of the Univ. of Vienna is, of course, for us of such historical importance that we are still very deeply shaken by the sad end of his life. The crimes of the Nazis are detestable. From the viewpoint of today, I can't understand how so-called men of culture who had a humanistic basis could be persuaded to commit such atrocities. This is not the right place to speak about these sad historical events.

Dr. Brosche's next words startled me:

The original score of Gustav Mahler's song "I Am Lost to the World" which Mahler gave to your grandfather as a gift for his 50th birthday is currently in the possession of Sotheby's Vienna.

A manuscript missing for half a century had surfaced in

Vienna just when I had started searching for it! For some reason, I felt sure that if I solved the mystery of what had happened to the Mahler manuscript, I would discover the real story behind my family's fate in wartime Vienna.

I immediately contacted Sotheby's attorney in New York and asked that a hold be placed on the manuscript. During my conversations with him, I learned the name of the person who had submitted the manuscript for sale. It was one that I had heard before: Richard Heiserer. This time it was Heiserer junior, a Viennese lawyer and son of the attorney who had represented my Aunt Melanie for about four months in 1941. How did my grandfather's property end up in the hands of the wartime attorney's son? It was suddenly clear that Heiserer senior must have played a larger role in my family's history than I had thought.

I learned that Heiserer junior had approached Sotheby's in Vienna in July within days of my learning of the manuscript's existence from Dr. Reilly. Heiserer had asked Sotheby's for an appraisal and was advised that it would fetch a higher price if it was auctioned at Sotheby's in London. The manuscript was valued at about $600,000, but Heiserer's plans to fetch top dollar from a private collector in London were foiled by the Austrian government. The Mahler was so precious that it was declared a national treasure that could not leave the country.

As I later learned, the Austrian government had asked Dr. Brosche, a few days prior to my e-mail to him, to help it decide whether the manuscript was a national treasure. That was why he knew exactly where the manuscript was. After ninety-five years, it had reappeared and its emergence was recorded across the globe in an amazing series of synchronous events.

Once I told Sotheby's that the manuscript had belonged to my grandfather, the auction house halted all proceedings and kept possession of the music until its ownership history— or provenance—could be cleared up. Sotheby's suggested I contact Heiserer junior to talk about the ownership of the manuscript. I received an e-mail on September 24 in which

Heiserer explained he had inherited the manuscript upon his father's death on August 17, 1957:

Because of my father's profession as a lawyer I start from the principl that he got Mahler's music piece in a legal way probably as compensation for his work he did as appointed lawyer to Dr. Guido Adler during hi lifetime or in consequence of his death. Besides I want to inform yo that my father had many Jewish clients and he helped at least ten Jew. to emigrate from Nazi Germany, i.e., Nobel [P]rize winner Dr. Otto Loewi and his wife. Therefore I don't accept your claim that you are th owner of Mahler's music piece and I won't agree to give it back to you

Heiserer had thrown down the gauntlet, and I had no choice but to take up the challenge. The Mahler manuscript had my grandfather's name on it, written in Gustav Mahler's own hand. It was known to have been locked in a vault in my grandfather's home until the Austrians welcomed the Nazis in 1938. Such a prized possession would not have simply found its way into the hands of an attorney. Did Heiserer senior really work on behalf of Jews during the war, implying he had no sympathy for the Nazis? The truth would turn out to be more ominous than his son wanted me to believe.

In October, I boarded a plane for Vienna planning to see with my own eyes the manuscript and the man who claimed it as his. For me, it was not only a legendary piece of music; it was a tangible link between me and more than 100 years of Adler family history that had been lost with the passage of time. That history began in the mid-nineteenth century in a small town in Moravia.

Chapter Two

GUSTAV AND GUIDO: THE EARLY YEARS

D r. Joachim and Franciska Adler had their sixth child, Guido, on November 1, 1855, in the little Moravian town of Eibenschitz, now a part of the Czech Republic. They were a pious Jewish family in what was then a German-speaking town. Joachim Adler was a country doctor and a leading advocate of homeopathic medicine. Although he had high hopes for his newborn son, he couldn't have known that Guido would end up as a world-famous professor at the University of Vienna where Joachim himself had graduated from medical school. Franciska, or Fanni, as the family called her, came from a Sudeten German merchant family who instilled in her a love of education that she would pass on to her children. Every day, Joachim bundled his medicines in a bag and hitched his horse to a buggy to make his rounds amid the farmers who often paid in kind, or not at all. Much like my own father 80 years later, Joachim lacked the talent for collecting money for medical services. Hard as he worked, he could not earn enough to ensure the financial security of Fanni and the children. He was widely respected and loved by the townspeople, who referred to him as *unser Herrgotterl* (our little God).

One year after Guido was born, his father contracted typhoid fever from a patient and died at the age of 48. Left with six children and no income, Fanni resolved to do the best she could for her children's future. She told her son later of a promise she made at her husband's deathbed. "Never," Joachim had said, "allow any of the children to become a doctor." So when later the teenage Guido mulled over his career choices, Fanni kept her promise and forbade him to follow the profession that indirectly had killed his father.

Fanni and Three of Her Children (Names Unknown)

Late in 1856, alone with two daughters, four sons and no funds to help feed and clothe them, Fanni pored over the ledgers her husband had left behind, hoping to collect at least some of the debts his patients owed him. Unsuccessful, she decided to leave Eibenschitz and move to the nearby town of Iglau where she could count on some help from her younger brother. Fanni could not have guessed that nearly 150 years later, a plaque would be placed on the house in Eibenschitz (now Ivancice) to commemorate Guido's birthplace. In Iglau, the family, which included Fanni's unmarried sister, settled down in rooms above a pharmacy facing the large town square.

Iglau Square — late 19th century

Iglau's history went back to the silver mines that had attracted merchants and fortune seekers to the banks of the Jihlava River in the thirteenth century. The town (now called Jihlava) was midway between Prague and Vienna in the Bohemian—Moravian highlands of today's Czech Republic. By the mid-1800s, its medieval aura had disappeared, thanks to a devastating fire and wartime destruction centuries before. When Fanni and the children arrived, the town was a jumble of architectural styles: Renaissance Italianate homes with galleries and frescoes, Baroque churches, and buildings with neoclassic facades. By then, Iglau's wealth no longer came from silver mining but from textiles, which the Empress Maria Teresa had supported in the town during the previous century. Because of its place in the multinational empire of Austria-Hungary, Iglau's townspeople—who gathered at the sandstone fountain of Aphrodite or beneath the column commemorating deliverance from the plague—spoke to one another in either Czech or German, and sometimes both within the same sentence! The multinational identity went still further with its mix of not only German and Czech speakers, but Christian and Jewish believers as well. The Jewish cemetery was founded in 1869, and Guido wrote in his memoirs that Catholics and Jews lived peacefully side by side. One of the Catholic churches sat next to a barracks that housed imperial soldiers. On the main street, the dashing young officers, "put the hearts of the young girls in a whirl," my grandfather remembered later.

Fortunately, living in Iglau became easier when Fanni received a *Gnadenpension*, a pension from the Habsburg Emperor Franz Joseph as thanks for Joachim's medical service during a deadly cholera epidemic years before. The grant allowed Guido and the other children to attend school, and there was even a little extra for all of the children to have music lessons with Johannes Brosch, a violin and piano teacher who would later give the young Gustav Mahler his first taste of music. Rabbi J.J. Unger cared for the Adler family's spiritual well-being while Fanni's youngest brother Bernhard, a merchant who would later marry his niece, was a lifelong mentor for my grandfather. The family lived a spartan life but achieved much with very little. Guido's three brothers would become successful later in life—one as a businessman in Milan, another as a lawyer and the last, as an actor who became director of the City Theater of Leipzig and the Court Theater in Berlin.

The success of the family can be traced to the strength and devotion of the widowed Fanni, whom my grandfather called "the best, most gentle and tender mother." As a young woman, she used to sing and accompany herself on guitar—an early influence on the blossoming musical interest of her son. But as the years passed, the hardship of raising six children alone weighed on her spirits. As Guido wrote cryptically in his memoirs, "Later on she didn't feel like singing anymore."

Fanni and the children left Iglau in 1864 and moved to the imperial capital of Vienna. Although there may have been several reasons for the move, it is likely that Fanni wanted her children to have the greater educational opportunities that Vienna offered. Fanni's decision was a boon to 9-year-old Guido as his musical interests emerged and ultimately transformed his life.

The culture shock must have been profound. Vienna was the fourth-largest city in Europe, the political capital of the Empire and a global capital of culture. Its streets teemed with immigrants from across the empire—men and women speaking Czech, Hungarian, Slovenian, Croatian and Italian. Those who spoke German borrowed sounds and words from other languages so that an accent, or a dialect, developed which was different from that in Germany. My grandfather may have grown up speaking this distinctively Viennese tongue, though it is more likely he spoke the Viennese of the educated classes, a grammatically correct, softly accented German.

Vienna's wide boulevards were lined with trees, and the elegant Baroque buildings four or more stories high were bejeweled with intricate stonework and statues. The fashionable Viennese gathered in the lush greenery of the Prater and rode on the new horse-drawn streetcars. Viennese ladies strove for the trim figure of the Empress Elisabeth, and the sprawling Hofburg boasted copper domes, gilded sculpture and the apartments of the imperial couple. As a child from a provincial town, 9-year-old Guido must have found Vienna larger than life.

Most important for my grandfather, Vienna was still the City of Music. It was there in the eighteenth century that Wolfgang Amadeus Mozart had written operas. In the nineteenth century, Vienna had hosted Franz Schubert, Ludwig van Beethoven, Johannes Brahms and Anton Bruckner. The Viennese elite danced in full regalia to the waltzes of Johann Strauss. The opera house was built along the famous Ringstrasse in 1869, and the Philharmonic gave concerts in theaters full of gilding and luxury.

My grandfather had excelled at his music studies in Iglau, though he wrote in his memoirs that he was never quite satisfied with himself. He did not have the creativity that makes for great musicians and composers. In Vienna, he attended the *Akademische Gymnasium,* a high school that prepared students for university, where he studied singing and conducted the opera choir. He also took classes at the famous Conservatory of Music. During the first year of his musical studies, he became so engrossed in the arts that his grades began to slip. Fanni put her foot down and insisted that her son must leave the Conservatory and concentrate on his academic studies. Terrified, Guido appealed to an advisor at the Conservatory, who told him to see a Catholic abbot named Helferstorfer for help. His knees shaking and report card in hand, Guido told the abbot his situation. The abbot glanced at the report card and took a long look at Guido. "My boy, I like you," he said, according to my grandfather's memoirs. "If you promise to fulfill your mother's desire to get better grades, you can keep your place [in the Conservatory]." Relieved, Guido gave his profuse thanks and dutifully delivered his report card to the abbot every semester to prove that he kept his promise. Music had taken a strong hold.

Because Vienna was the center of European music, Guido had the opportunity to encounter several outstanding composers during his student years. When Franz Liszt visited the Conservatory, Guido delivered a welcome speech on behalf of the student body. As thanks, Liszt kissed Guido on the forehead and grasped his hands. Guido kept the gloves he wore that night, describing them as "precious relics." The most profound meeting for Guido, however, was with Richard Wagner when the composer of the *Ring of the Nibelungen* visited a doctor at the General Hospital in Vienna. Guido and two colleagues carried an honorary trophy from the Conservatory for Wagner. When Wagner appeared, the students rose to their feet in a show of respect. Wagner told the students to study diligently because "without hard work the composer is lost. He first has to know his trade and only then can he follow his imagination." This meeting would not be Guido and Wagner's last.

Guido received an arts diploma from the Conservatory in 1874. By then he was in crisis: What would he do with his life? After years of studying music, my grandfather realized that he had the passion, but not the talent, to become a composer. He would later say that the decision was the hardest in his life. "I was and am of the opinion," he wrote in his memoirs, "that those who cannot contribute something new had better stay silent." This seemed to be my grandfather's version of the expression "Those that can . . . do, and those that can't . . . teach." Teaching was just one aspect of his eventual career choice; he would become a musicologist, a scientist in the service of music. The road to that decision was a winding one. He first thought of the father he had never known and considered a career in medicine, but the vow his mother had made on Joachim's deathbed stopped Guido from pursuing that path. Instead he settled on law, in which he found an outlet for his sense of social justice. He became active in law school, even proposing a new marriage law. He delivered a speech advocating the abolishment of the death penalty and wrote a play in which the heroine fought for the equality of women. (Many decades later I also worked on these issues as an attorney).

As Guido threw himself into law, music was never far from his mind. He began, on his own, to explore the history of music,

especially the works of Jahn, Chrysander, Spitta and Ambros,
as well as compositions before the seventeenth century. He
kept in touch with his music school classmates and launched a
venture that would bring him into contact with Wagner once
again, and into a lifelong friendship with the great composer
Gustav Mahler.

After finishing his law degree, Guido worked at a regional
courthouse. His legal career lasted three months, enough time
for him to realize that his future lay in the study of music history,
not in law. He returned to the university and joined Felix Mottl
and the medical student Karl Wolf to found the *Akademischer
Wagnerverein*, the Academic Wagner Club. Even before Adolf
Hitler adopted Wagner as the de facto Nazi national composer,
Wagner and his works were already controversial. His music
was dramatic, his operas reached back to German myths and
legends, and his productions took many hours to perform. In
his memoirs, Guido called it the Wagner Crisis, when Wagner's
"New German" music competed with what was accepted as
the time as classical music. Guido had been trained in the
classical style, so he approached Wagner with hesitation. He
began with the *Flying Dutchman* and moved through the works
until he reached the *Ring of the Nibelungen*. "The youth began
being carried away by an enthusiasm that finally swept me along
too," he wrote later. At first, the Academic Wagner Club
consisted of a group of young men who performed Wagner in
their rooms at night. But the club soon spread until it merited
its own meeting room at the *Akademische Gymnasium*. Guido's
family was astonished at his activities on behalf of the
controversial Wagner. Friends and acquaintances either
ridiculed him or expressed pity for his involvement. The club
tried to gather money for the festival theater being built for
Wagner spectacles in Bayreuth, but few donors came forward.
My grandfather saved what he could for the theater by lecturing
in music, an unreliable income at best. In the last days of the
month, Guido wrote in his memoirs, "I was happy with a
Knackwurst and a piece of bread." Yet these were some of the

best days of his life. He saved enough kronen to attend the first festival performance of the *Ring of the Nibelungen* at Bayreuth. Wagner spectacles would later feature Rhine nymphs in gauzy gowns who seemed to float over the stage (they were attached to iron poles maneuvered by men behind the scenes). But that first performance, as Guido described it, had little of the "overheated fantasy" that characterized later stagings. The music, however, touched my grandfather so deeply that after the show, he fainted at the door of his hotel room.

The next Thursday, Guido appeared by invitation at a party in Wahnfried—Wagner's home. Aristocrats and artists enjoyed the hospitality of Wagner's wife Cosima. Pretty young women surrounded Franz Liszt. Camille Saint-Saens sat at the piano and played his famous *Danse Macabre*. Anton Bruckner joined Wagner and Guido in a neighboring room. As Guido later recalled, Wagner said to him, "You seem to me a true art-loving young man; we must split the profits of the performance!"

My grandfather was in awe of this musical giant. Yet he mustered the courage to tell Wagner that during the performance, the text of the Ring was not always intelligible over the orchestra. The unpredictable Wagner could have blown up at the criticism, but much to Guido's relief, he agreed and blamed the singers. They would meet many times after this first Bayreuth festival. Guido would devote years to lecturing on Wagner, and would write one of the early studies of his operas. His familiarity with Wagner and decades of work on behalf of his compositions had consequences later. During World War II, his daughter Melanie appealed for help to Wagner's daughter-in-law Winifred. In her way, the avowed Nazi and wartime mistress of the Bayreuth Festival would have a part to play in the story of my grandfather's library—and the Mahler manuscript.

In 1877, the Wagner Club attracted one of its most famous members, Gustav Mahler. The 17-year-old was an honors student at the Conservatory, and friends with such fellow students as Hugo Wolf and Emil Freund who also made names for themselves as composers or directors. The musicologist Edward Reilly suggested that Gustav and Guido first met through the Wagner Club, despite the fact that the Adler and Mahler families both had lived in Iglau at roughly the same time. My grandfather's memoirs confirm that he had not met Mahler until the two were students in Vienna, but whatever the circumstances of their meeting, they developed a friendship that stuck for 30 years. According to Reilly, the youthful idealism of the late nineteenth century may have cemented the friendship, for Vienna at the time was a place where the "music dramas and writings of Wagner, the plays of Ibsen and the novels of Dostoevsky had produced a cultural climate that led many young men to devote themselves to art and to expect from art a regeneration of the world." My grandfather would retain this ideal throughout his life in his study of music. Mahler would live it in his compositions.

For the next eight years, Guido worked in Vienna on his theories of music history. The study of music as a science was known but not widespread. He would spend his life developing a method for classifying music, and creating a system for analyzing the historical development of musical elements. In 1885, he wrote an article entitled "The Scope, Method and Goals of Musicology." According to ethnomusicologist Bruno Nettl, Guido divided musicology into the historical and the systematic study of music, the latter of which examined "the bases of harmony, rhythm, and melody, aesthetics, music pedagogy . . . and comparative study for ethnographic purposes." Nettl found that my grandfather's article, still groundbreaking today, revealed how the young Guido Adler was a "firebrand, bringing to the world of scholarship a vision of a new field, musicology."

While my grandfather developed his theories, he also kept track of the blossoming career of the young Gustav Mahler. By age 20, Mahler had already completed a series of compositions, including *"Das klagende Lied"*, a *"Nocturne"* for cello (lost), a quartet and quintet for piano and strings (also lost), and a series of Lieder. Later, he conducted in provincial towns before becoming a choral director in Kassel in 1883. Wagner died early that same year, when both Gustav and my grandfather attended a performance of *Parsifal* at Bayreuth.

Though Guido was only five years older than Mahler, their early friendship took on a mentoring tone. In April 1880, my grandfather had asked his friend Franz Schaumann, later head of the Wagner Club, whether a post as choirmaster would be suitable for Mahler. Schaumann had replied that it was not, because the job "is less a matter of artistic ability than of a rather mechanical musician's experience." If Mahler took the job, he "would certainly be disillusioned in the first few weeks."

The first known direct communication between my grandfather and Gustav Mahler emerged in the few words written on the back of one of Mahler's calling cards which was found among Guido's personal papers. The card is not dated but probably stems from 1886. The exact words on the card are less significant than the fact that Mahler used the intimate German "du" form of the word "you," a convention reserved for close friends or family. It is worth stressing this linguistic point; a German speaker's use of "du" instead of the more formal "Sie" signals a close relationship. I discovered this myself in my own visits to Vienna. There was nothing quite like the astonishment of a Viennese waitress when I innocently but feloniously used the intimate "Hast du?" (Do you have?) rather than the proper "Haben Sie?"

In 1885, my grandfather became a lecturer at the German University in Prague. The academic structure at the time called for aspiring professors to spend years lecturing for little pay while publishing studies and developing a reputation. This work ethic suited my grandfather well but he became distracted long enough to fall in love with my grandmother, the Viennese Betti Berger. They had known one another since their high school days when they visited each other at home or met at

public dances. They married in 1887. My mother, Marianne,
remembered Betti later as a tiny woman who looked like a
bird with peculiar teeth. My mother loved her, but admitted
that she was "really ugly." But then, Marianne knew her only
later in life. Oil paintings of Betti done by her brother Ernst
Berger, a well-known portrait painter, belie my mother's
opinion, though it is possible that Ernst was charitable in his
renderings.

Guido and Betti — 1887

The Berger family was a well-to-do Viennese merchant clan.
Guido, the poor boy from Iglau, made a good catch in marrying
my wealthy grandmother. They would remain married for 50
years. On January 12, 1888, their first child Melanie was born.
Called Meli for short, she was a moody, brooding girl who would
grow up to be an eccentric member of Betti's kosher household.
On April 25, 1894, my father was born and given the name Hubert
Joachim, or Achim for short. His boyhood was surrounded by
music and the talk of music, and he dutifully took violin lessons.
The composer Johannes Brahms would visit the Adlers and play
waltzes on the piano for young Melanie and Achim.

Achim and Meli — 1896

Chapter Three

THE GIFT

A round the time of Guido's appointment to the university in Prague, Gustav Mahler was also there working at the German Theater. Guido had many opportunities to observe his friend's blossoming talent as an opera director. A draft version of an article my grandfather wrote about the German Theater in 1887 or 1888 spoke of Mahler as an element of nature, his work "youthfully fresh" and "stormy." At about the same time, he recommended Mahler for the post of director of the Royal Hungarian Opera in Budapest.

The friends also continued their friendship in the Golden City. Guido kept a guestbook, in which friends and visitors to his Prague home wrote short remembrances, snippets of music and autographs. On May 9, 1889, the Viennese musicologist Edward Hanslick wrote in the guestbook: "In grateful remembrance of the beautiful genial hours in the Adler home." A few weeks later, Mahler wrote a humorous poem that reflected his and Guido's awe at the visits of the great Hanslick:

Prague May 29, 1889

As long as we musicians linger in passing
Truly! we trembled before his epilogues!
Now, finally—at this place
—what a delight!—the last word was mine.
                    Gustav Mahler

Given Mahler's forceful personality, it's no surprise he sought the last word even in conversations with prominent men like Hanslick.

Edward Reilly found no documents linking Guido and Mahler between 1890 and 1897, though their friendship seemed to continue later with no mention of a break. During those years, my grandfather lectured in Prague, and until 1894, he edited the scholarly magazine he had helped found, the *Quarterly for Musicology*. He kept close contact with the Viennese music world by organizing the music portion of the music and theater exposition in Vienna in 1892. The early volumes of what would become the *Monuments of Music in Austria* were compiled by him in 1892 and 1893. At the same time, Mahler established his own musical reputation: as opera director in Budapest until 1891, when he took the post as director of the City Theater of Hamburg; as a composer who completed his Second and Third Symphonies (1894, 1896); and as conductor in London in 1892, and in Berlin, Moscow and Munich in 1897.

Later in life, my father wrote about my grandfather's days in Prague as the political situation between nationalities in Austria-Hungary deteriorated. Czechs resented the control that the German-speaking aristocrats from Vienna had over the politics and culture of their land. Many ethnic Germans called for a tighter cultural link between all German-speaking peoples no matter if they were in Bohemia, Germany or Austria. Germans and Czechs in Bohemia lived together only reluctantly, both groups pushing for dominance in their own language and culture. The social answer to this crisis was to keep Germans and Czechs separated. As an ethnic German, my grandfather was forbidden from befriending Czechs, according to the "German code of honor," as my father put it. Though Guido lectured in music at the German University in Prague, he could not openly go to performances at the Czech Opera House. To hear the works of Czech composers, he had to sneak into a dark corner of the theater so no one would recognize him. It was an omen of what was to come.

Gustav Mahler — 1892

Though Guido considered himself a Sudeten German—a German speaker from Bohemia—he believed throughout his life that all peoples were equal in the eyes of God, and that this equality should exist in the social and political spheres of all nations. His social liberalism, similar to the "One World" beliefs of French revolutionaries, went against the opinions of the time. As a German-speaking Jew born in a Czech area, Guido was a living affront to the nationalists who wanted all peoples to fit into tight linguistic, cultural and geographic boundaries. His liberalism became known during his tenure in Prague, and even Czechs slipped in to hear his lectures—including Thomas Garrick Masaryk, the future president of Czechoslovakia.

In 1898, the tension between the Czechs and the Germans exploded in Prague. Czech mobs roamed the streets beating Germans and looting their homes. The rioters soon arrived at the house where the Adlers lived. My grandfather's friendship with his Czech landlord saved Guido, Betti, 10-year-old Melanie and 4-year-old Achim from expulsion and beatings. When the mob asked if there were any German tenants, the landlord hung the Czech national colors on the house and informed the mob that only Czechs lived there. Guido sent his family back to Vienna the next night. "This was my first political flight," my father wrote later.

In October, my grandfather was appointed professor at the University of Vienna. There was much behind-the-scenes wrangling for the position, but Guido said nothing about it in his memoirs. As his friend Carl Engel wrote: "It was the mark of 'this humbly-proud man' that he would rather pass in silence over wrongs he had suffered than uncover the weakness or malice of his occasional opponents." A professorship in those days, as in Germany and Austria today, is a high honor that has as much to do with politics and influence as scholarship. Guido did not mention how he received this plum, only that he thrilled at the task of creating an institute for the study of music. He would never be rich even as a respected professor, but my grandfather approached his work "as a priest in the service of my ideals, and I would have exchanged places with no millionaire."

The Musicology Seminar of the University of Vienna came together with funds from the emperor, aristocrats interested in music, and private donors from as far away as Paris. It would grow quickly to prominence, its students and teachers among the best musicians, composers and scholars in the world. My grandfather referred to it as "my institute."

A year before, Gustav Mahler had returned to Vienna and had stepped into the highest position in Vienna's musical world: as director of the *Hofoper* (Court Opera), a position he would hold from 1897 to 1907, and the Vienna Philharmonic, which he conducted from 1898 to 1901. To help further his career, he had converted to Catholicism, an act some prominent Jews felt was pragmatic in Catholic Austria. His first performance was Wagner's *Lohengrin*. Mahler and my grandfather were both in Vienna again for the first time in 12 years, able to deepen their friendship on the same soil. But they were no longer students struggling to find their places in the world. Mahler virtually controlled the city's musical life as director of the imperial opera and the Vienna Philharmonic. Guido would teach or support the work of men who would revolutionize music and musicology, including Anton von Webern, Arnold Schönberg, Egon Wellesz and Rudolf von Ficker. The popular newspaper *Neue musikalische Presse* reported that many distinguished guests, including Mahler, attended Guido's first lecture on "Music and Musicology" at the university on October 26, 1898.

That same year, my grandfather helped Mahler publish his first work. Guido recommended that Mahler's first three symphonies be published by a Viennese printer. The expensive enterprise required a grant of 3,000 florins—funds that Guido found for his friend. The published scores, keyboard reductions and parts for Mahler's First, Third and a part of the Second

Symphonies launched his reputation as a serious composer. While most Viennese recognized Mahler only as a director, Guido compared his work with that of Richard Strauss, whose *Also Sprach Zarathustra* would become one of the most recognized musical works of the twentieth century.

Universities in Berlin and Leipzig copied Guido's model for an institute of musicology. His Musicology Seminar developed a fabulous library which, in 1908, consisted of 5,500 volumes. During my grandfather's 30 years as head of the seminar, 150 students graduated with doctorates in musicology, with countless others minoring in the subject or taking intensive course work. Roughly ten percent of his students were female. In his memoirs, my grandfather must have felt proud as he listed the achievements of his students: 9 composers, 6 directors, 28 music critics, 31 music teachers, 4 librarians and 1 dramatist. Nuns left their cloisters to study the history of church music at Guido's seminar. He wrote later, "God's blessings hovered over the institute."

Among musicology circles, my grandfather may be best known as the longtime editor of the *Denkmäler der Tonkunst in Österreich* (Monuments of Music in Austria). These volumes reproduced and preserved great music from the middle ages through the nineteenth century that arose from the territories of Austria-Hungary. For musicology students, the *Monuments* series was a treasure of centuries of Austrian music categorized and saved from obscurity. As editor, my grandfather received a private copy of each volume, and by the time he retired from work on the project, in his 80s, his collection reached 83 volumes.

Toward the end of the nineteenth century, Vienna reached its cultural peak—and began a political decline that would end in the disappearance of the empire. Freud explored the human mind in Vienna; Klimt and Kokoschka revolutionized painting. The horse-drawn streetcars of Guido's boyhood had become electric, along with the old gas street lamps. The giant

Ferris wheel from the 1873 World Exposition was the city's landmark, and Art Nouveau took the city by storm with its bold designs. The coffee houses, now the center of Vienna's cultural and intellectual life, were packed with customers—mostly men—reading newspapers or waving their hands as they talked. Art and politics were the topics of the day.

Despite its beauty and artistic vitality, fin-de-siècle Vienna decayed together with the empire of Austria-Hungary. Even as the Habsburg Emperor Franz Joseph watched his empire whittle away under military defeats and nationalist grumbling from subject regions, he still believed that his crown preserved the last vestige of the medieval Holy Roman Empire, and likened himself to the Roman-German monarchs, burdened with power over smaller, multiethnic and multilinguistic regions. Across the empire, political groups continued to agitate for union between German-speaking Austrians and the German "fatherland"—a sentiment the Habsburgs themselves would have endorsed had it not meant giving up the monarchy. As the empire came apart at the seams, and political power in the years leading up to World War I shifted away from Vienna to cities on the periphery such as Prague and Cracow, both Franz Joseph and the average Viennese in the Prater sensed that their best days—and Vienna's—were coming to an end.

The Viennese fought the fatalism of the day with *Gemütlichkeit,* a way of life that favored enjoyment. My grandfather later wrote, "In many respects the Viennese are like the ancient Romans: *novarum rerum cupidi* (they are fond only of new things)." The Vienna he and his friend Gustav Mahler knew was full of hedonism and gaiety, smugness and apathy.

In this beautiful, decaying city, the friendship between my grandfather and the musician deepened as Mahler rose from opera director to recognized composer. Mahler planned a private performance for Guido of his *Second Symphony* on piano, and the friends talked of "a little bicycle excursion in the

Dolomites in the next few days," as Mahler wrote to Guido in August 1900. Guido attended a performance of Mahler's *Second Symphony* in Munich later that year, and afterward met up with Mahler, Mahler's confidante, the violinist and memoirist Natalie Bauer-Lechner, and others at the Park Hotel for drinks and a discussion of the response to Mahler's work. My grandfather clipped newspaper articles and reviews of Mahler's performances, and saved theater programs in his private papers.

Then in 1901, Mahler composed a song: "*Ich bin der Welt abhanden gekommen*," or "I am Lost to the World," based on a poem by German poet Friedrich Rückert (1788-1866). That summer, he had composed parts of two series of songs based on Rückert poems, the first a five-song cycle called the "*Kindertotenlieder*," or "Songs on the Deaths of Children." Its melancholy lyrics revealed Mahler's preoccupation with the darker moments of life, six years before his own beloved first child Maria Anna died of scarlet fever. The second set of songs were released as five separate songs that are now commonly performed together as the *Rückert Lieder*: "*Blicke mir nicht in die Lieder*," "*Ich atmet' einen Linden Duft*," "*Um Mitternacht*," "*Liebst du um Schönheit*" and finally "*Ich bin der Welt abhanden gekommen*," ranging from carefree melodies to love songs to expressions of weariness.

Mahler's songs, written either for orchestra or for voice and piano, were by no means lesser musical forms than his symphonies. Rather than pit symphony against folk song, Mahler worked to fuse the two. My grandfather thought that the songs "embrace nature, the world of children and adults in the most diverse moods of love, profane and sacred, the most complete devotion descending by degrees to resignation, which achieves expression in the most luminous manner in the incomparable '*Ich bin der Welt abhanden gekommen*.'" Natalie-Bauer-Lechner said that "*Ich bin der Welt abhanden gekommen*" nearly didn't get written at all. As summer came to a close, Mahler had finished several Rückert songs and had made a start on the Fifth Symphony. He wanted to enjoy his last few days in the bucolic Austrian countryside "when he was suddenly seized with the urge to set the last of the *Rückert* poems that he had originally planned to do, but set aside in favor of the *Symphony*. This was "*Ich bin der Welt abhanden gekommen*."

Ich bin der Welt abhanden gekommen	*I am lost to the world*
Mit der ich sonst viele Zeit verdorben	*with which I used to waste so much time,*
Sie hat so lange nichs von mir vernommen,	*It has heard nothing from me for so long,*
Sie mag wohl glauben, ich sei gestorben!	*That it may very well believe me dead!*
Es ist mir auch gar nichts daran gelegen	*It is of no consequence to me,*
Ob sie mich für gestorben hält	*Whether it thinks me dead;*
Ich kann auch gar nichts sagen dagegen,	*I cannot deny it,*
Denn wirklich bin ich gestorben der Welt.	*for I really am dead to the world.*
Ich bin gestorben dem Weltgetümmel,	*I have died to the world's tumult*
Und ruh' in einem stillen Gebiet!	*And rest in a realm of quiet.*
Ich leb' allein in meinem Himmel,	*I live alone in my own heaven,*
In meinem Lieben, in meinem Lied!	*in my love, in my song.*

Mahler said later that "this song, with its unusually concentrated and restrained style, is brim-full with emotion but does not overflow." The *Rückert* songs were first performed for orchestra on January 29, 1905, and Mahler had them published individually that year. Thus "*Ich bin der Welt abhanden gekommen*" had already circulated in Vienna when Mahler decided to give my grandfather the original handwritten score that would become one of his most precious possessions.

Guido Adler — 1905

On November 1, 1905 my grandfather turned 50. Graying hair formed wisps around a bald crown, and sideburns led to the luxuriant beard he would wear the rest of his life. Round spectacles perched atop a long, rather bulbous nose. But it was the eyes—slightly squinting but clear as water—and the deep lines between them, that showed his love of study. Guido's face was not stern, though as a prominent professor at the University of Vienna, he was expected to remain distant from his students. Instead, a kindness showed through. He had the face of a mentor, or at the risk of sounding redundant, like a favorite grandfather.

Although it is unknown exactly how he spent his birthday, the numerous birthday cards that still exist in his personal papers show how many visitors there must have been to help the famous professor celebrate. Guido's coffee breaks always included a cake piled high with whipped cream, and there is no reason to think he ate any differently on his birthday. Birthday dinner would have included Guido's favorite dishes: boiled beef with horseradish or pig's knuckles, with the pastry Kaiserschmarren sweetened with honey or powdered sugar for dessert. What *is* known is that some time during Guido's birthday, Gustav Mahler appeared with a present. They hugged, Mahler kissed my grandfather's bearded cheek and presented his gift—the handwritten orchestral score of "*Ich bin der Welt abhanden gekommen.*" The bundle of pages, lined with severe music staffs, began with a dedication in Mahler's quick, sloping hand: "To my dear friend Guido Adler (who will never be lost to me) as a memento of his 50th birthday."

No one knew of the personal dedication until 80 years later, when Reilly discovered a reference to it buried among my grandfather's papers in Georgia. "That Adler carefully refrained from mentioning this gift in any of his published writings on Mahler may give some indication of his feelings about publicizing personal relations in his historical work," Reilly wrote. "He refers to it only in an unpublished Nachwort [afterword], originally written to conclude his [Mahler] study of 1913 when it was issued in book form in 1916, but he subsequently discarded this afterword in favor of the briefer and less personal Vorwort [preface] found in the published volume."

By 1905, Guido and Mahler had been friends for 30 years—from their days as students among the Rhine maidens in the Academic Wagner Club to their lives as leading lights of the Viennese music world. They hadn't always seen eye to eye, and may have long indulged privately in good-natured envy of one another. My grandfather referred to Mahler as "a master of our time" for his skills as a conductor and director, and for the brilliance of his compositions. Mahler joked about Guido's pleasant life as a scholar. In a letter to his wife Alma in 1904, Mahler commented on Guido's newly published study of Richard Wagner: "Oh that I were a Professor of Music and could give lectures on Wagner and have them published." It is easy to imagine the tortured composer envying the satisfying life of the scholar, while the scholar envied the raw creative passion of the composer. Perhaps the sarcasm indicated the disparity in their outlook on music. My grandfather sought the links between music scholarship and composition, but Mahler doubted that the academic, without direct experience of music composition and performance, could truly understand it.

Whatever their disagreements, Mahler and my grandfather had remained friends, and *"Ich bin der Welt abhanden gekommen"* was a gift that reflected the endurance of that friendship. It was far from simply a memento. Mahler had finished five symphonies and many orchestral songs, yet had said of the song, "It is my very self!" World weary yet intense, emotional without sentimentality, the song that Mahler gave Guido was the song closest to Mahler's own personality, and it was like giving away a part of himself. Though in 1905 Mahler was more famous as a conductor than a composer, he must have realized that one day the autographed manuscript might become a valuable collector's item.

Certainly, my grandfather knew it, for he kept it locked in a vault in his home for the rest of his life. He wanted to preserve the memory of his friendship with Mahler, of course, but perhaps he also wanted to shield it from fire or water damage. No harm should come to a musical score by a composer who Guido knew was brilliant, and whose time would come.

Gustav Mahler — 1907

That time, however, proved to be short. In 1901, Mahler underwent surgery for a hemorrhage that forced him to take a sick leave. Though he promised Guido that he would allow younger conductors like Bruno Walter to take over some of his heavy workload, Mahler jumped back into the fray almost immediately after recovery. The year of crisis was 1907. He traveled constantly, directing concerts in Berlin, Frankfurt, Rome, St. Petersburg, Wiesbaden and Helsinki. Then came the tragedy of his life in July: His daughter Maria Anna died of scarlet fever. To add to his grief, the festering heart disease that had plagued Mahler for years was finally diagnosed. He also lived in fear that his amorous wife Alma would leave him. The strain showed in his work. At a performance of Schoenberg's *Chamber Symphony, Op. 9*, Mahler demanded silence from an audience that protested the new music by noisily scraping back chairs or leaving the hall in the middle of the concert. Mahler's furious stance offended the Viennese public, which prided itself on its musical taste. Worried for his friend, Guido telephoned Alma to comment on the scandal: "Gustav made a painful exhibition of himself today. May cost him his job . . ." Mahler left it on his own accord. He conducted his last performance at the Vienna Court Opera and left Vienna in December.

My grandfather watched the deterioration of his friend, but was helpless to stop it. The last years of Mahler's life were spent traveling between Europe and the United States, and the two probably had little time to meet alone. Mahler's wife, Alma, complicated the situation by keeping her husband shielded from his old friends. Alma generally did not like the older men like Guido who influenced Mahler. Guido may not have realized this at first; Alma kept up the appearance of civility, even writing him in 1909: "I have learned that you have the feeling that it might have been my intention to alienate you from Gustav! I am immensely sorry! In this entire year— which is now finally past, I have experienced such terrible oppressiveness—such a chain of sorrows—that I was shy—of every person with whom I had not yet spoken—from fear of losing my laboriously won self-control!! Thus it happened that we seemingly neglected you and your dear wife." She closed the note by saying that Mahler wanted Guido and Betti to visit the Mahler family.

Mahler spent three seasons conducting at the Metropolitan Opera House in New York and the New York Philharmonic, both lucrative positions. His move to America was controversial to his old friends who could see that Mahler's health suffered under the strain. Guido suspected that Mahler's grasp at the brass ring in America came at the urging of Alma, who wanted a more luxurious life than they could afford. In 1910, Mahler wrote a letter to my grandfather trying to dispel the rumors about his ill health and Alma's financial pressure. He insisted that he was not overworked as he had been in Vienna, that his health was better than ever, and that his wife had only his health, not extravagance, in mind. He explained that he wanted money for himself to augment the scanty pension he had received after decades as a director and composer. "And are we perhaps obligated to eat the charity bread of the Vienna Court Opera in a garret in Vienna?" Mahler asked. "Should I not, inasmuch as it is offered me, in a short time earn a fortune in honorable artistic work?" Mahler's frankness was a testament to his friendship with my grandfather, which survived misunderstandings that reached to the heart of Mahler's life and family. Though this letter was published in the 1924 collection of Mahler letters released by Alma, Guido claimed he had never received it.

Midway through the concert year in 1911, Mahler's health finally failed him. He traveled to Paris for a last-minute cure but it was too late. He returned to Vienna and died around midnight on May 18. He was buried next to his daughter. My grandfather rarely inserted emotion into his public writings, but he made an exception in the unpublished *Nachwort* written for his 1913 study of Mahler:

Even before the day of his last, disastrous voyage to America . . . into which the almost mortally exhausted man was driven by others for the sake of the mammon that he scorned—he came to me, pale, with weary eyes, and spoke the words, incomprehensible to me at the time: "Whatever may happen or put itself between us, we remain old friends in our inmost relations." Later, the "mortally weary man came back mortally ill, and his noble soul departed into another world—different from that new one suggested to him. At that time I obtained his promise: "Gustav, you must never again go to America." He promised, and kept it, as in life every promise was sacred to him.

Autograph Page — *I am Lost to the World* by Gustav Mahler

Chapter Four

1911 TO 1938: YEARS OF CHANGE

The years after Mahler's death in 1911 saw a transformation of Guido's Vienna and Austria-Hungary as a whole. The empire crumbled from within but still fed its craving for crowns by annexing Bosnia and Herzegovina in 1909. Five years later, the Austrian heir apparent Archduke Franz Ferdinand died after an attack by Serbian nationalists. The Emperor Franz Joseph delivered an ultimatum to Serbia, which was rejected. Russia backed Serbia against the Austrians, while the German Kaiser Wilhelm promised Austria his full support. On July 29, Austrian troops attacked Belgrade. By August, the Great War had begun.

Vienna celebrated what would become its last grasp at imperial glory, but my family was uneasy from the beginning. An underlying reason for the war was the nationalism that sprouted across Europe at the time—Czechs, Romanians, Hungarians, Croatians and Serbians fighting for independence from their principal European overlords, Austria and Russia. Jews founded their own nationalist movement, Zionism, at the same time. At first, Guido accepted the nationalist arguments, but his philosophy later evolved into one favoring the equality of humanity over national, ethnic or linguistic origin. Like many intellectuals of the time, he would look to internationalism, socialism and communism as an alternative to nationalism.

My father recalled later that the Zionists labeled Guido with the worst word in their vocabulary—assimilationist— because he would not support their nationalist agenda. As World War I broke out and young men across Austria-Hungary were mobilized, Guido looked on as my 19-year-old father put on a uniform to fight in a war whose principles he would come to doubt.

Achim (Far Right) at War — 1916

My father interrupted his medical studies to enlist in the army. Guido noted in his memoirs that his son had wanted to fight instead of serving as a medic. In 1893, the Austrian army had begun a balloon corps and Achim joined it as a reconnaissance man floating above the battlefield, observing troop movements. Whenever enemy soldiers took potshots at this floating target, my father retaliated by dropping grenades or whatever heavy objects he had on hand. Although never wounded, he had lifelong kidney problems, which he always claimed had been caused by sleeping on the wet battlefield. He returned to Vienna at the close of the war in 1918.

The defeat of Germany and Austria-Hungary in World War I sealed the fate of the empires. Franz Joseph had died in 1916 and his grandnephew Karl had become the last emperor of Austria-Hungary. Once the war was lost, Karl watched his empire dissolve into new independent countries—Yugoslavia, Czechoslovakia, Hungary, and Romania. Austria shrank to its present size, a shadow of its former self. Defeat spelled economic as well as political chaos for what remained. Vienna, the beautiful and proud capitol, was now head of a small, defeated country cut off from its old imperial resources and drained of funds that had disappeared in the war effort. In the 1920s, as an economic crisis gripped Austria and brought widespread unemployment, inflation, poverty and hunger; the socialists took power in Vienna.

Hard times in Vienna touched everyone, though Guido's university salary continued to support the family. But his professional pride and joy, the *Monuments of Music in Austria*, almost came to an end for the simple reason that the new Austria no longer had paper to print on. My grandfather appealed to Thomas Masaryk who, 20 years before, had listened to his lectures, and had since become president of the new Czechoslovakia. Soon after, a carload of paper arrived at the plant where the *Monuments* volumes were printed.

Middle-class families in Vienna fared worse than the Adlers. The Fischmanns, whose daughter Marianne would become my mother, was headed by my grandfather Otto, a socialist banker reputed to have a photographic memory for stock market figures. After World War I, his motto, "Take care of the pennies and the rest will take care of itself," no longer worked. The family's livelihood evaporated. There was so little food for 12-year-old Marianne that the government sent her and many other children to Denmark where there was enough to eat. The organizers of the trip knew her only as a number on the tag of her dress, another hungry child in a group of hungry children on a train going north. My mother remembered that 20 children slept in a train compartment built for six. Some of the children had lice; soon all of them did. My mother's lifelong aversion to travel began on that claustrophobic, lice-infested journey.

Though the 1920s were a dark time for the Austrians, Guido met a man whose friendship would be crucial to the Adler family in later years. Carl Engel was head of the Music Division at the Library of Congress in Washington, D.C. from 1922 to 1934. He was an Austrian who had lived in the United States since 1905 and became a citizen in the last year of World War I. Engel and my grandfather became friends while at a Beethoven centennial festival in 1927. Afterward, they kept in contact through correspondence and met once again only when Engel returned to Austria in 1930 to help the Library of Congress with a special acquisition—a Gutenberg Bible owned by the monastery of St. Paul in Carinthia.

There only as an interpreter, Engel used the opportunity to meet my grandfather in Klagenfurt, the town where the final negotiations would take place. When Guido appeared at the Klagenfurt train station, Engel remembered, "We embraced, and from that moment on I was no longer lonely." He described Guido as walking with an elastic step and holding bubbly conversations in his racy Viennese vocabulary. If the fancy hit him, my grandfather stopped people of all ages and backgrounds in the streets and talked to them about whatever occurred to him. Joined by Librarian of Congress Herbert Putnam, they finally glimpsed the perfectly preserved Gutenberg Bible at the monastery. Engel saw tears stream down my grandfather's cheeks. That moment would always remain magical, and the friends, despite living on different continents, continued their visits and letters for the rest of my grandfather's life.

Guido and Carl Engel at St. Paul Monastery

In those years, Guido continued to show his devotion to Gustav Mahler. He was honorary guest at the Mahler Festival in Amsterdam in 1920, where his delight at the performances of Mahler's music mingled with his observations of the Netherlands' wealth compared to the poverty of Austria. Two years later, Guido helped Fritz Egon Pamer complete the first doctoral dissertation on Mahler's work, "Gustav Mahlers Lieder." In 1926 and at Guido's suggestion, the newly formed Gustav Mahler Monument Committee began planning how to raise money for a monument to the composer. After more than a decade of disagreement over the design of the monument and where it should be located, the committee was forced to hand over the funds it had raised to the Nazi government which took power in 1938.

By the 1930s, my grandfather Guido had achieved far more than what could have been expected of a poor boy from the provinces of a lost empire. The musicology department at the University of Vienna had been his lifelong work, and serious students of musicology had Guido's books *Style in Music* (1911), *Methodology of Music History* (1919) and *Handbook of Music History* (1924) on their shelves. Centuries of great Austrian music lived

on in his more than 80 volumes of *Monuments of Music in Austria.*
He still had the medals and honors that the old imperial order
had bestowed on him for his work, and he carried the
prestigious imperial rank of Hofrat.

The Hofrat Professor Doktor—though no one would call him
by all of his titles at once—retired from the university in 1927,
and his beloved wife Betti died in 1933. Without Betti's strong
hand over the household at Lannerstrasse 9, my grandfather
increasingly relied on his daughter Melanie. Following in her
grandfather Joachim's footsteps by studying homeopathy at the
University of Innsbruck in the 1930s, she is said to have been the
first woman to receive a medical degree from that school. Her
own family, with the possible exception of her father, saw Meli as
a strange bird. After her degree, she never settled anywhere,
never worked, had few or no friends in Vienna and lived separately
from the family—but in an unknown location—until she moved
in with Guido in 1938. She was always "going away" to Munich,
Graz, or one of the many spas in the countryside, and no one in
the family knew why. She may have been seeking a cure for one
of her mysterious and possibly imagined ailments.

Meli (Far Right) with Colleagues

Yet she always returned to Lannerstrasse 9, and no one in the family doubted her devotion to my grandfather. Now in his seventies, Guido spent more and more time at his home—a villa two stories high in the fashionable section of Vienna called Döbling. My grandfather may have chosen to live in this northeastern edge of the city because of the rich nature nearby: the Wienerwald lush with lindens, chestnuts, deer and wild pigs, and the vineyards where Veltliner grapes grew near the banks of the Danube. When he wasn't working on his memoirs, *Wollen und Wirken*, which were published in 1935, Guido often took walks in the parks and forests or stopped by a *Weinkeller* in autumn for a glass of the young vintage Heurige. Döbling, which was also known for its "cottage" section, was an upscale neighborhood of classically designed stone homes with gardens or grounds. Lannerstrasse 9 was such a home. Guido's study was the focus of his house. A large window near his desk faced the garden, bookshelves reached from floor to ceiling, a grand piano supported stacks of books and music. Over the years he had created a library filled with thousands of letters and books (some inscribed with affectionate notes from their famous authors), musical manuscripts, academic studies and other private papers.

Guido in His Library

To make some sense of the avalanche of material, my grandfather enlisted the help of an assistant, musicologist Carl Rosenthal, who catalogued the library in the 1930s. The full catalogue has been lost, but an abbreviated inventory gives a glimpse of its value at the time. My grandfather owned a complete and partial set of the *Monuments of Music in Austria*, an incomplete set of the *Monuments of Music in Germany*, a complete edition of Beethoven music, a letter collection and the autograph orchestra score of *"Ich bin der Welt abhanden gekommen"* by Gustav Mahler. The inventory was taken before 1938, because the values attached to the items were in Austrian schillings, not German Reichsmarks. The total came to 23,000 schillings (about $4,347 at the 1938 exchange of .189 schillings to the U.S. dollar or $55,730 in present U.S. dollars). Rosenthal wrote later that he had never seen the Mahler manuscript probably because it was always kept locked in my grandfather's safe. For years, Guido had planned to write a biography of Beethoven, thus many of his books and materials related to the composer. He even owned one of the three authentic death masks of Beethoven.

It is easy to imagine Guido's cultured musical home as an oasis against the political and social changes of the 1930s that would eventually destroy Austria. In its shrunken, post-war condition, socialists dominated Vienna's politics while the provinces remained parochial and conservative. Red Vienna, as it was sometimes called, was accurately looked on as a haven for Jews, since after the dissolution of the Habsburg empire, Jewish refugees from the former imperial provinces arrived there en masse. In the early 1920s, Jews formed more than 10 percent of the population, but unlike the prosperous Viennese Jewish professionals like my grandfather, the newcomers were workers or small tradesmen who competed with the average Viennese for work. In a post-war environment of high unemployment and inflation, non-Jewish Viennese of all social classes, ages or political stripe blamed the Jews for their economic misery. And their sentiment was not ignored by unscrupulous politicians.

This feeling was nothing new. For decades, political groups from German nationalists to clerics to democrats hammered out their own positions on the "Jewish question"—whether Jews who converted to Christianity were no longer Jews (a religious definition of Jewishness), or whether one was a Jew from birth till death despite religion (a racial definition). The Viennese gift for vagueness meant that politicians used whichever definition suited them at the time, which allowed antisemites to favor some prominent Jews or Jewish converts to Christianity while at the same time castigating working-class Jews to win the political support of non-Jewish voters. The opportunistic Karl Lueger, controversial mayor of Vienna in the last years of the empire, declared, "Wer ein Jud ist, bestimme ich" (I decide who is a Jew).

Adolf Hitler's definition of a Jew never strayed from the racial camp. He won election as German chancellor in 1933 on a platform based on nationalism, economic development, military readiness and antisemitism. Almost immediately, the Jews of Germany lost most of their rights. The German electorate listened to, and largely believed, Hitler's explanation for the loss of World War I: The Jews had betrayed the Reich. Hitler promised to help Germany regain its national pride by ripping to pieces the Versailles Treaty, which had hobbled the country in 1918. Article 80 of the treaty, which sought to prevent another alliance between Germany and Austria by demanding that Germany respect Austria's independence, incensed Germans and Austrians who longed for unity.

Austria without its multinational empire considered itself thoroughly German in a cultural sense, and throughout the 1920s and 1930s, the nationalist groups which favored a union between the two countries gained in popularity. Although they were not strong enough to win political elections, the Nazis had a presence in Austria before they took hold in Germany. After Hitler took power, nationalist Austrians ignored or applauded his antisemitism and hoped that the Nazi wave would hit Austria.

Still more heartbreaking for my grandfather Guido, the vanguard of Nazism in Austria flourished among the students of his beloved university. The universities in Austria had been considered "inviolable territories" where even police could not enter. The downside of this autonomy became clear when German nationalist students transformed the universities into "Brown Houses"—referring to the brown shirt uniforms of the Nazis—by harassing Jewish students and professors even when Austrian law forbade it. The police refused to help.

Austrian law did forbid the harassment of Jews, while German law under Hitler mandated or condoned it. The reason for this difference lay with the relatively weak fascist chancellors of the Austrian Christian Social Party in the 1930s. Engelbert Dollfuss and Kurt Schuschnigg rallied under a flag that symbolized Austrian Catholicism, and were outspoken in their right-wing agenda, but they were not German nationalists and wanted to preserve Austria's independence from Germany. Austrian Nazis, on the other hand, worked to unite the countries, eventually assassinating Dollfuss during an unsuccessful putsch in 1934. Although the Christian Socials did not allow Jews to be beaten or slandered, nor did they condone organized efforts to deprive Jews of their homes and property, they did run a repressive regime in which political opponents of all stripes were imprisoned. As historian Robert Wistrich noted, "Their authoritarian Christian state ideology did bring with it a quiet discrimination against Jews and the first erosion of Jewish emancipation in seventy years . . ." It was the beginning of the end for Jews in Austria.

Chapter Five

DECISIONS

On March 12, 1938, Guido read the headlines in the nation's censored newspapers: Germany's Eighth Army had crossed the Austrian border the night before. Photographs show Austrian border guards grinning as they lifted the barriers to allow the Germans through. During the days that followed, Austrians clogged the town squares to celebrate the union with Germany. When Hitler's black Mercedes sped along Austria's roads, Austrians gathered behind to take clumps of earth "blessed" by the Führer. History would call this the Blumenkrieg, or Flower War, based on how happily the country gave up its sovereignty. On March 13, Hitler declared the Anschluss—Germany's annexation of Austria—official.

My father followed the news with dread. He was now a doctor in private practice with only a nurse and not much to do. Eight years before, he had moved with his new bride, my mother Marianne, into an apartment on Gonzagagasse in central Vienna that doubled as his medical office. The day after the Anschluss, my father was 44 years old, a stocky man

Austrian Border Guards, March 12, 1938

Hitler Speaks to Austria, March 15, 1938

with thick, wild eyebrows, thick glasses and a large, smooth skull framed by graying hair. My mother, 14 years younger and eight months pregnant, was a classical pianist trained at Vienna's Conservatory She was a beautiful young woman who had never lacked admirers before she married my father. My sister, Evelyn, was a 7-year-old strong-headed child.

As he followed the momentous events of March 1938, my father thought of the safety of his growing family. The aftermath of the First World War made it clear that an alliance between Austria and Germany meant chaos and destruction. Twenty years after the Treaty of Versailles, his kidney trouble continued along with a distrust of politicians and a conviction that his children should not have to endure the deprivation that he and my mother had endured. Therefore, the morning after the Anschluss, my father visited my grandfather Guido, 82 years old and increasingly frail, at the villa on Lannerstrasse. Achim later wrote that Guido looked disgusted as he sat at his desk reading the newspaper. "It makes me sick to read this Nazi stuff," he had commented, "but I have to read a newspaper don't I?" Then Guido added, "I guess I will not sit in the box [reserved for members at the Music Society theater] from now on." A year later, his suspicion proved correct. In a letter from October 26, 1939, the president and vice president of the Friends of the Music Society of Vienna stated:

Pursuant to the new statutes of our society, which we have enclosed, you are informed that according to paragraph 5 of the statutes, the confirmation of your honorary membership will not be conferred.

It is not difficult to envision the effect that this letter had on a man whose life had been spent at the center of Vienna's musical life. In 2002, I wrote to the society asking for my grandfather's honorary membership to be reinstated. The society responded that it would not do so, because today's society was not responsible for what the Nazi-era organization had done. It was a denial of responsibility that I would often encounter in Austria.

My father had long before concluded that Guido was politically naive, despite the fact that he must have had sufficient political skill to secure public support and private endowments for the *Monuments of Music in Austria* and his Musicology Seminar at the University of Vienna. Perhaps his political sense was outdated or idealistic, or perhaps he was merely tired. He and my Aunt Melanie thought the Nazis would come and go, and Austria would return to normal. Instead, the world of Austria's Jews was coming to an end. On the night of March 13th, the Gestapo began systematic looting of Jewish property. It confiscated anything valuable and shipped the spoils to Berlin. Many Austrians soon got into the act by participating in beatings, public humiliation of Jews and destruction of businesses. Jubilant Viennese blocked streetcars as they crowded the promenades and city squares. The crowd cheered an end to the "exile" of Austrians whose destiny, they believed, belonged with the German Reich. Hope radiated from the faces of ordinary Austrians, hope for a future of national pride, strength and prosperity—everything they lacked after World War I. Hitler had voiced what many Austrians had long believed: that the Jews had stabbed Germany and Austria in the back and this betrayal had cost them their victory in the Great War. Some Austrians who did not support Hitler, the Anschluss or antisemitism were arrested; others kept their beliefs to themselves.

Jews had never been wholly secure in Austria, but now even the cultured Viennese dropped all restraints in their persecution of their Jewish neighbors. They could do what they wanted to the Jews and fear no consequences. Paper swastika flags appeared as if out of nowhere, thousands in the hands of the people, waving like a red sea. Hitler Youth hurled abuses at the Jews lined up at government offices to get the documents they needed to leave the country. Jewish men and women were forced to scrub anti-Nazi graffiti off the sidewalks with their coats and scarves, or with toothbrushes. Jewish shop owners could only watch as Austrians broke their store windows and painted the word "Jud"—and sometimes "Dachau"—for all to see. Mobs organized by the Nazis damaged the Great Synagogue of Vienna, which was later occupied by German troops.

Meli in Library

Some days after the Anschluss, my Aunt Melanie opened one of Guido's desk drawers and discovered a cable from his

old friend Carl Engel, who had left the Library of Congress and was now president of the G. Schirmer Inc., a music publishing company in New York. Melanie showed the March 13 cable to my father. In it, Engel pleaded with Guido to flee Austria with his family. Engel volunteered to sponsor the entire family and support them in America, an opportunity he was in a good position to offer. Aside from his post as head of Schirmer's, Engel was an honorary consultant in musicology to the Library of Congress, editor of the *Musical Quarterly* and a founder and president of the American Musicological Society. In essence, Engel's telegram was an offer to save my grandfather' life—a second time. The first time had been in 1930 in Liège when Guido was an energetic 75-year-old. As Engel remembered it, he and Guido had strolled down the street on the way to their hotel, my grandfather sauntering along, umbrella in hand, his eyes on the sky in search of stars in the daylight. An oil truck lost control and barreled down on Guido. Engel grabbed him by the coat collar and pulled him to safety. Fortunately, the only thing my grandfather lost was a shoe, found later under the truck. When he and Engel returned to the hotel for a settling glass of cognac, my grandfather had tears in his eyes. "We must hereafter call each other Du," he said to Engel, referring to the intimate form of the German word "you." "The last man I asked to call me so was Gustav Mahler."

Eight years later, Engel offered himself again in the role as guardian angel, but my grandfather—perhaps unsure that the political situation warranted such a drastic move—had hidden the cable from his family. My father, however, made his decision quickly. With a baby along the way, mobs destroying Jewish homes and businesses, and with Jewish offices already closed down by the new government, the only option in his eyes was emigration. Guido could hardly believe the news. Over the next few days, my father tried to convince Guido and Melanie that they, too, should leave. The bitter truth wasn't easy to swallow. The family would become refugees. There was no guarantee they would be granted asylum in the United States because like Britain, France and so many other countries, it had strict quotas on the number of Jews allowed from Germany. As the summer wore on, flight would be even harder; in July, delegates from 32 countries who attended the Council of Evian in France declared that their nations had reached the saturation point, allowing more Jews through their borders was impossible. The council signalled the world's unwillingness to open itself to all of the Jewish refugees who needed asylum. In the end, the United States and Britain took in the majority of refugees.

My father knew that leaving Vienna would mean the loss of his home and possessions, his relatives, the status he had enjoyed as the son of Guido Adler, his professional standing and his entire history. My father's World War I veteran status would count for nothing. My grandfather's role as a founder of musicology and the titles, medals and honors that came with his life's work would be almost worthless in New York. My Aunt Melanie wasn't married and had no friends the family knew of, but she, too, would lose her own peculiar way of life. These were the negative sides of emigration. But if they didn't leave, the losses would be even worse. After the Anschluss, all of the anti-Jewish laws in Germany were enacted in Austria in one massive sweep. The Nazis called for a general ban on Jewish businesses. The first deportations of Jewish bankers and businessmen left for Dachau. Jewish social organizations such as sports clubs were banned. By the early days of the war, some 500 Jews would escape deportation by committing suicide.

For a time, Guido and Melanie were convinced. They went to the U.S. Consulate to get their quota numbers. My grandfather returned a second time for a medical exam. The consul tried to make the process as easy for the Adlers as he could; every eminent scientist that went to America would be a plus for the United States. If Guido had still been working as a professor, he could have left Austria almost immediately on a non-quota visa. Because he was retired, he had to wait for his number to come up along with the rest of the family.

Guido Adler — Visa Photographs — 1938

On April 10, Austrians across the country thronged to their voting precincts. Hitler had called a national referendum with only one question on the ballot: Should Austria be annexed into the German Reich? Guido, Achim, Marianne and Melanie would have voted "no!" if they'd been allowed to vote at all. As it was, no Jews or other "undesirables" could cast their vote on the fate of Austria. Voter turnout was high, and the results almost unanimous: 99 percent of eligible voters (almost 4.3 million people) approved of joining Hitler's Reich. A full 12,000 Austrians dared to vote no, despite the intimidation of Nazi flags hanging over the ballot boxes and Gestapo stationed outside. The victors of World War I—Britain, France, the United States—who had forbidden the union of Germany and Austria, looked on and did nothing.

In the United States, Engel had filed an affidavit supporting my family's applications for entry visas. He understated my family's reason for leaving Austria as "on account of racial problems." Unknown to Engel, his desire to help Jews emigrate initially coincided with the wishes of a Nazi whose name would become particularly infamous—Adolf Eichmann. An arrogant young Nazi, Eichmann worked on his home turf. He was an Austrian entrusted with the task of making his country *judenfrei*, free of Jews. At first, emigration was the official policy for "cleansing" Austria. Under Eichmann's thumb, the Jewish community mobilized almost exclusively for emigration, with offices set up to help with the paperwork and the funds to pay the taxes the Nazis required. Eichmann demanded that Jewish organizations help 20,000 poorer Jews emigrate in the first year after the Anschluss. He smugly reported in a memo to a colleague, "They promised me that they would keep to this." Only later would Eichmann and the German Reich decide that emigration was not the solution to the "Jewish Question."

Letters flew between my father, my grandfather and Carl Engel in New York. Guido wavered, unsure whether he could really go through with emigration. He was 82 years old and had lived in his home for 40 years. With his university pension, his forests and wine houses of suburban Vienna, and his library of treasures acquired over the course of his life, he was troubled by the idea of relying on Engel for his very existence. Engel tried to comfort him. He offered to pay for everything, to move to a larger apartment in New York, to take Guido to Maine in the summers for the forest walks Guido loved. Melanie mirrored her father's feelings, vacillating between leaving and staying. In his brief account of those days, my father wrote little about what Melanie really thought, only that she followed the will of her father. If Guido stayed, she would. If he went, presumably she would too. As Melanie and my grandfather waited for their quota numbers to come up, their desire to emigrate weakened.

Perhaps they wavered because my father abruptly left. As one of their scare tactics, the Nazis rounded up Jewish professionals at random. When the Gestapo hunted for Jewish doctors, my father went into hiding at the Hotel Panhans in Semmering, a spa town southwest of Vienna. For a few weeks he left my mother to manage the paperwork for emigration— passports, medical certificates and travel arrangements. She would talk later of waiting hours in line at the emigration office, her unborn baby kicking, in hopes of getting one more signature, stamp or necessary piece of paper. It was not easy, as the Nazis often changed the rules of emigration without notice. There was always one more stamp or signature to be had, one more form to fill out.

I was born on April 24, 1938. My father had returned from hiding in Semmering to be beside my mother and me at the hospital. After my mother's sister Lisl visited us, Achim paid for her taxi ride home. It had become too dangerous for a Jew to walk alone in Vienna.

Three days later, the Nazis ordered all of the Jews in Austria with assets greater than 7,500 schillings (about $1,418) to fill out a 4-page form, in triplicate, listing property, loans, mortgages, jewelry, art collections and business equipment. The Austrian authorities needed the inventories in order to tax Jewish property as accurately, and as thoroughly, as possible.

Assets had to be listed according to their purchase value, no
the actual price at which they could be sold. With the pressure
on Jews across Austria to sell everything from houses to
businesses, the prices were bargain basement for any buyer of
"Aryanized" assets. Even today, "Aryanized" artwork appear
for sale in the antique shops and auction houses of Vienna.

Guido, Achim and Melanie filled out their assets forms in
July, and laid bare their financial situations just before the war
My Aunt Melanie, who had never worked, had more money
than her father or brother—nearly 90,000 Reichsmarks in assets
(about $36,144 at the 1940 exchange of 2.49 Reichsmarks to
the dollar). With slightly more than a half share in the house
on Gonzagagasse and a quarter share of the Lannerstrasse
home, as well as assorted Austrian and British bonds and funds
Melanie did well on paper. No one in the family knew where
she got her money, although her parsimonious nature, coupled
with her father's lack of funds, suggests that he had given her
money over the years. My grandfather had almost nothing. His
house on Lannerstrasse, his scanty pension from the university
and a small savings in the bank came to just over 21,000
Reichsmarks. He didn't include an inventory of his personal
library, or estimate the value of his music collection, which
included the gift from Gustav Mahler. My father Achim, a
working doctor with a wife and two children, had just over
60,000 Reichsmarks in total assets, mostly from his half of the
Gonzagagasse home. He wrote on the forms that he had only
25 Reichsmarks in cash. This was no surprise because of the
frantic preparations for the move to the United States. But all
of the preparations meant nothing if he couldn't pay the various
taxes the Nazis demanded, which came to about half of his net
worth. The *Reichsfluchtsteuer*, the tax on Jews fleeing abroad,
amounted to 20,000 Reichsmarks alone—money my father
didn't have in cash. The family's quota numbers could have
come up at any time, but Achim had to pay the tax before
boarding the train that would take the family to a ship in
northern Germany. The two pieces of debt my father listed on

his asset form could explain how he paid for at least a part of the taxes. Melanie had loaned him 10,600 Reichsmarks as a mortgage on the Gonzagagasse house, for which he agreed to pay 7 percent interest. He borrowed another 2,912 Reichsmarks from his mother-in-law Ida Fischmann. In an update to the Nazi authorities a year later, Guido also wrote that his assets had dropped by several thousand Reichsmarks, partly to help with "the emigration of my son Dr. Hubert J. Adler."

On August 5, 1938, the quota numbers of our family finally came up. Out of the things my mother and father had acquired over their eight years of marriage, my sister Evelyn's toys, my baby things, and the equipment of my father's liquidated medical practice, we could carry only what fit in a few suitcases. The day before our train was scheduled to leave, my parents visited my maternal grandmother, Ida. As Ida's other daughter, my Aunt Lisl, told the story years later, Achim hoped Ida wouldn't ask for specific information about their departure to America. My grandmother was an emotional woman, and displays of emotion made my father uncomfortable. Eight years before, he had proposed to my mother, not by going down on one knee with flowers, but by handing her a paper covered in numbers and asking, "Do you think we could make a living on this?" Thus my father advised my mother not to tell Ida the family was leaving the next day. He fell back on his medical training to explain why they should avoid such an emotional moment. Ida looked frail from worry over the Anschluss, he told my mother, and would be better able to handle the shock of their leaving if they were just suddenly not there. My mother agreed, but she must have been reluctant. She had great respect for her husband's medical judgement, but she still felt a certain unease with his reasoning. So Ida Fischmann had no idea we had left until Melanie called her a few days later. My grandmother would never see us again. My parents never talked about the departure, whether they said goodbye to Guido and Melanie at Lannerstrasse, or whether they all gathered at the train station, together until the last moment. I

would like to think that there were hugs and many tears
Perhaps they kept up the hopeful fiction that they would mee
again when Guido and Melanie's quota numbers came up anc
they, too, crossed the Atlantic.

We climbed onto a train that steamed out of Vienna anc
two and a half hours later, reached the German border. The
journey continued eight hours straight through Hitler's Reich
to Bremerhaven on the northern coast. The rest of the trip
would be made by ship, but customs officials held up the long
lines of refugees in a meticulous search for anything of value
Only the most resourceful people succeeded in smuggling
jewelry or large amounts of cash out of the German Reich,
most had sold everything they had to pay for exit visas and
transportation. My mother told me later that a customs official
had asked her to undo my diaper, an ideal place for contraband.
As the official leaned closer, I urinated on his face. Years later,
my mother relished telling this story over and over again; to
her, my act contained some small act of revenge.

Once cleared through customs, we boarded the SS *Bremen*,
a passenger liner that took us over the Atlantic to New York
Harbor. My grandfather Guido and Aunt Melanie stayed
behind in the familiar rooms of Lannerstrasse 9. Their quota
numbers came up and expired. Guido couldn't bring himself
to leave. "The old Adler has grown tired of flying," he told his
friend Mosco Carner. It was a play on the name Adler, the
German word for "eagle."

Chapter Six

THE VULTURES CIRCLE

My family had joined the more than 100,000 Jews who streamed out of Austria before the war started, leaving my grandfather and aunt among the fewer than 60,000 Jews who stayed behind to test their fate under the Nazis. Any illusions of safety they may have had disappeared within three months of our departure. On the night of November 9, 1938, the Reich-wide night of terror known as *Kristallnacht* (Night of Broken Glass) descended on Vienna. Attacks on Jewish businesses, schools and synagogues had taken place in Austria ever since the Nazis took power, but it reached a degree of frenzy in November. In one night, 49 synagogues and numerous prayer houses were destroyed. Nearly 4,000 Jews were sent to Dachau and Buchenwald until they could prove they intended to emigrate. As the Simon Wiesenthal Center has pointed out, pogroms against the Jews in Germany were a bureaucratic affair, while in Austria, persecution was like "street theater," enacted by ordinary Austrians . . . or old acquaintances.

The day after Kristallnacht, the Gestapo arrived a
Lannerstrasse 9 accompanied by one of my grandfather'
former students, Alfred Orel, then librarian of the music histor
department at the University of Vienna and director of the
music collection of the Library of the City of Vienna. The
Gestapo searched the house for Jewish dwellers while Naz
Party member Orel concerned himself with a more lucrative
issue—he wanted the valuable music library Guido had buil
up over 60 years. Carl Rosenthal, my grandfather's assistant
witnessed Orel directing the confiscation of part of the library
which, at the very least, included the 83 volumes of *Monument
of Music in Austria*. It was a day, Rosenthal wrote later, "that
shall never forget." The Nazis left my grandfather in his home
because of his age. The sections of the library Orel left behind
would fall under the control of the Gestapo, which entrusted
the key to the room to a Viennese lawyer with a checkered
past—Richard Heiserer. Six decades later, Heiserer's son would
suddenly appear at Sotheby's Auction House in Vienna with
my grandfather's Mahler manuscript under his arm.

How did my grandfather feel at this invasion of his home
and confiscation of his scholarly treasures by one of his former
students? He left no letters with a direct reference to the
confiscation, but from other letters of that period, it is clear
that he suffered from depression, probably owing to concern
over the fate of his family in America and the worsening
conditions in Vienna. Just before Kristallnacht, Melanie had
written Marianne and Achim, "Please don't write any more
sad letters to father." Achim had written about his difficulties
adjusting to life in the United States, where he had no money,
no medical license and an accent that marked him as
German—a potential enemy if the United States should enter
the war. Two days after Kristallnacht, the German Reich
imposed a collective fine of one billion Reichsmarks on all Jews
still living in the Reich. This *Judenvermögensabgabe* (JUVA) was
a 25 percent tax on Jewish assets—yet another organized
economic bleeding of the Jewish population. The Nazis

characterized the tax as an "act of atonement." My grandfather and Melanie had to update their financial forms. On November 29, Guido listed his total worth at 18,052 Reichsmarks (RM), nearly 5,000 RM less than in July. He wrote on the form that part of this money had been used to help his son emigrate, and part had been used to pay his own bills. The JUVA tax my grandfather had to pay was calculated in 1939 as 4,200 RM. He appealed that number, stating he should owe only 3,027 RM. According to Melanie's update on the tax forms, her JUVA tax was levied at 24,300 RM in 1940. She disputed the amount because her total worth, as reported on her November 1938 form, had dropped by 25,000 RM to 63,800 RM. The steep dip in her total worth was due partly to the general devaluation of Jewish property at the time.

The bills piled up at Lannerstrasse 9, and Melanie could do little about it. The Nazis forbade Jews to work. In October 1938, Melanie wrote to my father about what she and Guido owed for the telephone and ironing, small worries that my family had never had. Guido must have felt that yet another important part of his life—Achim and the grandchildren, his beloved university, his library and now his economic security—was disappearing before his eyes. Melanie was his only comfort. To her own family, she remained an enigma. "The complete nut of the family," my mother Marianne recalled later. Melanie was 50 years old in 1938. None of the family photos show her smiling. Her dresses were plain, her face without makeup; she was the unglamorous opposite of Marianne. Her personality and way of life were things the family simply couldn't understand. She made no close friends in Vienna, never married, and had no fixed home in the city except for her father's house. A long and mysterious sickness plagued her so that "she always took her little pills and her little stuff," as my mother said later. Melanie never looked sick, my mother recalled, but she would go to "certain spas" to take a cure. For reasons he never expressed, my father intensely disliked his sister.

Melanie (Meli) Adler

Melanie's lifestyle was cause for rumor in the family. Marianne recalled later what Betti had said about her daughter: "She does certain things we're not talking about." What things? My Aunt Lisl, who was my only other relative to leave Nazi Austria, offered a possible clue years later when she voiced one of the family rumors. It seems that when Melanie and Achim were children, they had a governess they called Fräulein

Reiss. Achim had told Lisl later that Reiss was rumored to be a lesbian and that somehow Melanie was involved. Melanie herself added fuel to the story by occasionally wearing a man's hat and trench coat, and by traveling twice a month to Munich, then a center for the homosexual community.

Melanie's alleged lesbianism was kept well underground. And it is possible that some of Melanie's peculiarities could be explained quite differently. My Aunt Lisl thought that Melanie didn't want to look Jewish and had no Jewish connections. For decades, intellectual Jews had often brushed off their Jewishness, defining themselves according to religion rather than race or ethnicity, which they could then ignore or even change, as Gustav Mahler had. Though Betti had kept a kosher household at Lannerstrasse 9, neither Melanie nor my father became religious as adults. Perhaps Melanie, because of shame or self-preservation, sought to minimize her Jewishness by avoiding her family's community in Vienna, where her Jewish father was so well-known. In Munich or Graz, she could reinvent herself. As Marianne—who liked Melanie—said later, "I wouldn't be surprised if she tried to join the Nazi Party." The anti-Jewish explanation, of course, reamins as much speculation as the lesbianism. A homeopathic doctor and a hypochondriac, an unmarried woman who wore men's clothing, a 50-year-old with no known income but substantial assets, a Jew with antisemitic tendencies—Melanie was and will always be an enigma.

The only clues to the life of my grandfather and Melanie for the rest of 1938 and in 1939 spring from letters they wrote to my family in the United States. My father suspected that at least some of the family letters had been confiscated by the Nazis before they could reach the States, but Guido rejected that theory. On Dec. 3, 1938, he wrote his son, "Either you or Marianne had this fantasy that maybe letters did not arrive; it is quite possible that one or another might get lost during the journey." In 1939, Guido's notes became shorter, his handwriting so tremulous that it was sometimes difficult to read.

"Father is healthy but has grown very old, not as much in a physical sense but in a mental sense," Melanie wrote to Achim in February. He "speaks often in half sentences and has almost no memory left." Again she urged her brother to help her shield Guido from any bad news. "He's very upset about how things are going with you and I beg you that when there is something to complain about, don't inform him about it." Guido had received a letter from a family friend in Amsterdam with a photo of the man's mother who, Melanie discovered, had committed suicide recently. "I am keeping that secret from father," she wrote to Achim.

Before my father's birthday in April, Guido wrote: "This old man would like to look in the future, but it is not possible. But he is filled with hope. God will protect you—this is my daily prayer. This goes for my daughter as well. We pray together." In mid-May, Guido commented on his healthy habit of taking an hour-long walk every morning and afternoon through the cottage section of Döbling. Melanie added her own comments to the letter: Guido had been so glad to receive Achim and the family's latest letter that he read it over and over again. She had placed a photo of me that my parents had sent her in the frame of her bedroom mirror.

On May 21, 1939 Guido sent Achim a handwritten copy of his last testament:

In full possession of my mental powers and free from any pressure I set up my last will as follows: As sole heir to all of my possessions, in whatever form they come, I name my daughter Dr. Melanie Adler. My son Dr. Achim Hubert Adler has no more claim to his legal part of my estate because he has already received his due portion as payments in advance.

Presumably, the portion of the estate my father had received had taken the form of financial help to flee Austria. On January 4, 1940, my grandfather filed a codicil to his will that transferred the publication rights of his books and articles to Achim. By the time my father could claim the legacy after the war, the publication rights were worthless.

On September 1, 1939, German troops invaded Poland and World War II began. Later that month, my grandfather wrote to Achim that Melanie was spending two weeks working in Munich. He didn't mention what kind of work she did or for whom. In October, Achim wrote an upbeat, chatty note to his father that seemed to fulfill Melanie's plea to tell Guido only good news. "As you can see from the picture, the kids are happy and contented, which is the most important thing," my father wrote. "All of us are doing well, and we hope the same for you. Eva is making good progress in school and Tommy will soon be in kindergarten." Guido dusted off his English in a birthday note to my sister Evelyn: "Best wishes for your birthday. I embrace you and hope you will good learn." The day after Christmas 1939, Guido thanked his son for sending Christmas wishes, another indication that the family was not strict about religion. Along with good wishes for the new year Guido wrote back "Yes, we live in difficult times."

By 1940, the 60,000 Jews who remained in Vienna found their lives more difficult than they could have imagined. "They were mostly unemployed, evicted from their homes and living with other families, crammed into 'collective' apartments, their bank accounts blocked or frozen," according to a report of the Committee for Jewish Claims on Austria. "In short, they were barely surviving."

Unlike most Viennese Jews, Guido still had his home and his pension. But although his life was more sheltered, he was not altogether shielded from the changes in his country. Some time after the Anschluss, a Nazi Party leader was assigned to live on the first floor of the house on Lannerstrasse 9. He felt a certain pity for the elderly Guido, and when my grandfather collapsed outside during a walk, it was the the Nazi who found him and carried him back to his bedroom. On another day, the police arrived at Lannerstrasse 9 with orders to arrest Guido.

The Adler family's longtime housemaid warned the policeman that Professor Adler was 85 years old. The policeman left and never returned.

Yet as time wore on, my grandfather turned in on himself, isolated in his home. As Carl Engel remembered later, he had lost contact with his friends and stopped writing the letters that for decades had been his main connection to music scholars, composers, philosophers and other friends around the world. He grew too feeble to take his daily walks. On November 6, 1940, just after his 85th birthday, he wrote to Achim: "I am living a very secluded life with my daughter, taking delight in your well-being." It would be Guido's last known letter. Even before he left for America, Achim had known his father's health was failing. Guido had suffered from insomnia for 40 years, combating it with sleeping potions that had taken their toll over the decades.

By January 1941, he was close to death. Melanie wrote to Achim later of their father's last weeks. "Slowly, death crept in," she wrote. "Good days alternated with bad days. A light flu, then a pause, then a slight stroke with paralysis in the legs. Within 24 hours, nearly everything was okay again." The two comforts during my grandfather's last days were his daughter's presence and his house on Lannerstrasse 9. But Austrian Nazis prepared to strip him of the home he had lived in for decades. Not long after the Anschluss, the Nazis had ordered all Jews in Austria to move to Vienna. Later, Jews had to crowd into Leopoldstadt, Vienna's 2nd district where there had once been a Jewish ghetto. That Guido and Melanie still lived in a nice home on the outskirts of the city was unacceptable to the Nazis.

In January 1941, a regional court in Vienna ordered my grandfather's eviction from Lannerstrasse 9. On January 15, an attorney by the name of Adolf Leischner wrote to Professor Erich Schenk, the new chair of the Musicology Seminar at the University of Vienna: "I would be very grateful to you, dear professor, if you could furnish me as soon as possible with an expert evaluation about the scientific importance of the achievements that Prof. Adler has rendered to the University of Vienna, as well as his standing in world opinion." Leischener closed the letter with "Heil Hitler." Schenk replied to Leischner the next day that "Although it is repugnant to me to give an expert opinion on a full Jew," Guido Adler's distinguished academic career and worldwide reputation was something to be reckoned with. "Considering the high opinion of Adler by people in countries favorable to Germany, I think that the delogation [i.e., eviction] of the said person would definitely create an unfavorable impression on Vienna, its university and the department that I represent. It is one's duty to point out the consequences of this." My grandfather was allowed to remain in his home.

Though a group of Guido's friends and students had in the past worked successfully to keep Guido from being evicted, Schenk would later tell Melanie that he alone prevented the court from evicting her father. Although Melanie initially believed him, there may well have been a far more influential intervention by Richard Wagner's daughter-in-law Winifred Wagner, a close friend of Adolf Hitler and an avowed Nazi. Though a convinced National Socialist, Winifred did not support Nazi violence and often tried to help those whom her party persecuted. It is quite possible that she contacted Leischner and asked him to look into the Adler case. This theory is supported by a letter Winifred wrote to Melanie on January 17th :

Dear Frau Adler,

I have taken steps to spare your aged father from eviction, but I have no idea if an exception to the law can be made here. I will inform you of an answer.

With best greetings,
Winifred Wagner

In February, my grandfather's health worsened. Though we were in America when Guido lay dying, my father wrote later about what he had heard from others about Guido's last days. My grandfather's thinking was confused, and he would "utter incoherent sentences, looking for people that weren't there and talking to them." Melanie wrote to Achim that their father would wander at night in the darkness. "Then he became bedridden and didn't want to eat anything." Several days before Guido's death, Melanie fell into a mysterious "deep unconsciousness," as she wrote to Achim. Marianne said years later that her mother had written to her that Melanie could not take care of Guido anymore. The implication was that Melanie had gone to Munich or elsewhere as her father lay dying. Whatever the real story, Guido Adler died in bed on February 15, 1941 at the age of 86, apparently of natural causes.

Bizarre as it may sound, Melanie wrote that she "woke up" from her "deep unconsciousness" only after my grandfather was already cremated and his urn placed in the Vienna Crematorium. Guido was not laid to rest beside his wife Betti, as he had wished, and no newspaper obituary appeared to mark the passing of one of Vienna's most prestigious music scholars. For decades, my family in America didn't know where Guido was interred. In 1981, his urn was located by a group of his colleagues who exhumed and buried it in an *Ehrengrab*, a grave of honor, in Vienna's Central Cemetery. The choir of St. Elisabeth Church accompanied the solemn ceremony, which was attended by prominent musicologists and professors of the University of Vienna. My father, who died in 1964, had not lived to see Guido finally honored.

Chapter Seven

EMERGING SELF-INTERESTS

After Guido's death, my Aunt Melanie was virtually alone. We had fled to the United States nearly three years before and Melanie had only some extended family and friends left. Once recovered from the mysterious ailment of February 1941, she awoke as the sole heiress of her father's small but still significant estate. The house at Lannerstrasse 9 was hers, but more importantly for her future, she now possessed my grandfather's valuable library.

Of course, Melanie couldn't claim her inheritance without moving through the local probate court system. Shortly after my grandfather's death, the Nazi attorney Richard Heiserer appeared on the scene ostensibly to represent her in the probate proceedings. Exactly how this representation occurred is unknown, but the evidence suggests that Melanie did not accept Heiserer's representation of her own free will. Guido and Melanie had several attorneys they had turned to for help in the past. Melanie had been represented in matters involving her property by an old family friend and attorney, Dr. Leo Reiss, who also represented her mother Betti. Another Viennese attorney, Dr. Robert Peltzer, had also represented the family. In addition, Guido's brother-in-law Alfred Berger was an attorney with whom Guido consulted on several occasions. The probate record indicates that as of January 14, 1940, still another attorney in Vienna, Dr. Walter Redlich, had apparently prepared and was in possession of Guido's will.

Heiserer may well have forced himself on my family by taking advantage of the edicts that forbade Jews from practicing as lawyers. On April 10, 1933, Germany passed the Law on the Admission to Legal Practice, which forbade the admission of Jews to the legal profession. On April 24, 1934, the German Ministry of Justice forbade Jewish lawyers to serve as public defenders for an "Aryan" client. On August 31, 1934, acting in his capacity as Hitler's personal representative, Rudolf Hess forbade lawyers belonging to the Nazi party to represent Jews in court. Finally, on December 2, 1934, the whole issue of Jewish attorneys was put into a concise Reich Attorneys' Ordinance: It reiterated the existing ban against the admission of Jews into the legal profession and forbade Jews from using the title of attorney-at-law (*Rechtsanwalt*). As though these weren't enough, on September 27, 1938, the Fifth Decree Governing Reich Citizenship Law was enacted. It stated:

Section 1. The profession of lawyer is closed to Jews. In so far as Jews are still lawyers they are eliminated from the Corps of Lawyers in accordance with the following regulations:

In the Province of Austria: Jewish lawyers are to be stricken from the list of lawyers at the latest by December 31, 1938, by order of the Reich Minister of Justice.

Obviously, only "Aryan" lawyers like Heiserer were able to practice law.

Even before the German army entered Austria in 1938, Heiserer had proven his dedication to the Nazis. The Nazi Party was banned in Austria under the Schuschnigg government, but Heiserer worked on behalf of party members who landed in Austrian courts. He defended Hubert Eisner, head of the illegal Nazi Party branch in the province of West Styria, and in 1937, he stepped into a more sensational case: Nazi Party member Urban Knollmaier had been accused of blowing up the Lieser Bridge, for which the prosecuting attorney demanded the death penalty. Heiserer succeeded in reducing the sentence to life in prison, an achievement the Nazi authorities did not forget once they took power in Austria. Unemployed Nazis were able to find work on Heiserer's properties in West Styria, further evidence of his support for "party comrades." He joined an auxiliary branch of the Nazi Party in July 1937, but apparently didn't pay his membership dues. On November 22, 1938, he finally applied for full party membership and landed on a waiting list on September 27, 1940. Like all non-Jewish attorneys, he also joined the attorney branch of the Nazi Party, and his letterhead displayed both its symbols: the swastika and the eagle. A Nazi Party district report from 1943 or perhaps later commented: "[Heiserer's] conduct toward the party and the state is impeccable. He spent a lot for the party, and eagerly. His personal assets are very substantial. He behaves socially to the other party comrades."

In 1939, Heiserer shifted his legal representation from Nazis—who no longer needed it—to more lucrative clients. Jews needed lawyers to help them navigate the jungle of new anti-Jewish laws. Apparently owing to the Hess directive that forbade "Aryan" lawyers from representing Jews, special permission had to be obtained to acquire Jewish clients. Heiserer repeatedly requested this right. In September 1939, Heiserer wrote in a party memo that he was advising the Nobel Prize winner in medicine Dr. Otto Loewi and his wife as to

how they could liquidate their assets to pay the exorbitant taxe
the Reich demanded for Frau Loewi's emigration (her husband
had already emigrated). The Jewish couple had given Heisere
power of attorney, which he noted was "in the fiscal and
economic interest of the German Reich," a phrase he repeated
in many of his requests. The Loewis eventually reunited abroad
without a penny left to their name. After the war, Heisere
would tell a denazification commission that he, too, was
hindered by the Nazis: The party didn't allow him to
represent Jewish clients in a case that would have bagged
him 80,000 German Marks. Clearly, Heiserer's motives for
representing Jews were not altruistic. With so many
regulations allowing the confiscation of Jewish goods, an
attorney appointed as executor of Jewish estates had virtually
a license to steal, since an attorney would be given the keys
to Jewish residences in order to conduct inventories. The
opportunity for self-dealing and theft was real, and Jewish
clients had no recourse.

Antisemitic sentiments, as well as the laws that allowed
"Aryans" to enrich themselves, encouraged many lawyers to
choose loyalty to the Reich—or their own pocketbooks—over
their clients. Hermann Goering called on all Nazis to deprive
Jews of their assets in a process "according to our laws legally,
but mercilessly followed." This mandate threw lawyers into the
forefront of "Aryanization" efforts that were designed to appear
legal under the twisted laws of the Nazis. After the first
spontaneous seizure of Jewish property died down in the weeks
after the Anschluss, a more efficient bureaucratic apparatus
run by party leaders, the police, tax authorities and lawyers
sprang up to assure that Jewish assets went to the Reich. In his
dealings with the Loewis, Heiserer showed himself a significant
instrument of this apparatus. Melanie quickly learned that her
attorney represented interests other than her own, but
fortunately, she had a loyal family friend who *did* work on her
behalf.

Rudolf Von Ficker

Rudolf von Ficker was born in Munich in 1886, the son of a prominent historian. He studied musicology under my grandfather in Vienna, then founded the musicology institute at the University of Innsbruck, where he specialized in Medieval and Renaissance music. He returned to Vienna to teach music history and to work on the *Monuments of Music in Austria* from 1927 to 1931, the years directly following Guido's retirement. During those years, Ficker helped reawaken an appreciation for

Medieval music by staging concerts in Vienna. At the time of my grandfather's death in 1941, Ficker taught musicology at the University of Munich. During the war, the Gestapo harassed him and his wife because of their anti-Nazi stance. Unlike other professors, for example, Ficker refused to accept student paper bearing special marks next to Jewish sources. And no major work even if written by a Jew, was to be neglected in the research of Ficker's students, though it was common for German scholars at the time to suppress Jewish academic achievements. Ficker's outspokenness hindered his career, as he wrote after the war: "I calmly accepted my lack of promotion, a salary cut, exclusion from the National Science Institute of Berlin, from the Reich and state 'Monuments' . . . I was also boycotted by specialty journals (*Deutsche Musikkultur, Musik*). In none of these will you find a single line written by me in all these years."

Thus, the old family friend Rudolf von Ficker was a natural advisor for my Aunt Melanie when the Nazis threatened to steal her inheritance. Professor Erich Schenk, head of the Musicology Seminar at the University of Vienna—my grandfather's old position—had a keen eye on Guido's library. Though it had been "repugnant" to him, Schenk had written a letter of recommendation that had helped keep my grandfather from a Gestapo-ordered eviction from his home. Schenk's was by no means the most influential voice in the case; former students and colleagues, especially those with connections to Governor Baldur von Schirach, had banded together to keep the Gestapo from Guido's door. Somehow, however, Melanie was led to believe that it had been largely Schenk's doing that allowed her father to die peacefully at home. She revealed her gratitude and desperation in a brief but fateful letter to Schenk written between February 15 and March 10, 1941:

Dear Professor,

Hardly had everything been resolved to the best with your kind help at the end of father's life when he passed away gently and painlessly.

*I myself have been unconscious for days because of a severe flu.
Now I awoke again to my hunted life. I keep thinking how it
might be possible with your kind assistance to get to my Aryan
relatives in Italy.*

*We talked about that theme at that time, and now it would be
of the most acute importance to come to the fulfilment of this
matter. It is merely a matter of getting there. My relatives would
then take care of me. Could you please advise me as soon as
possible and come to my assistance?*

*With my cordial regards and the wish that you might be able to
help me.*

Dr. Melanie Adler

Schenk's response to my aunt's plea hinted at what was to
come. He suggested that she leave Guido's library to the
Musicology Seminar at the University of Vienna in exchange
for an exit visa to Italy and 5,000 Reichsmarks. Melanie then
visited Ficker in Munich on March 11 and asked his advice on
Schenk's offer. As Ficker wrote later: "I told her that at least 90
percent of all works were already in the possession of the
[Musicology Seminar] library and that she would have to face
the possibility that the books would end up being distributed
in different places. I recommended finding a buyer who would
keep the complete library together, so that she could claim it
later. I also recommended that in addition to a small monthly
payment or suchlike, she should aim at getting a letter of
protection." When Melanie returned to Vienna she informed
Schenk that it was no deal. Schenk, however, was determined
to enrich the Musicology Seminar and enhance his own
reputation. Had Melanie known anything at all of Schenk's
background, she might have foreseen his later actions to
confiscate the library with the help of the Gestapo and Heiserer.

Erich Schenk — 1956

Erich Schenk was born in Salzburg in 1902 and studied music theory and piano at the Mozarteum. In 1925, he received his doctorate in musicology at the University of Munich after studying under a critic of my grandfather's Viennese school of musicology. He subsequently went on to study music under Guido and other professors, and in 1929 he completed what was required to become a professor at the University of Rostock. Schenk founded Rostock's musicology department in 1936, and left for Vienna in 1940. The promotion from an obscure university in northern Germany to the famous Viennese

Musicology Seminar was suspect, according to Schenk's post-war critics who claimed he had done little to distinguish himself in musicology. Supposedly, the Education Ministry under the Nazis had appointed Schenk to the post in part because of his knowledge of Mozart and Gluck.

Egon Wellesz

But there was more to Schenk than the professorial. My grandfather's former student Egon Wellesz, who would help Ficker investigate Schenk after the war, wrote that former Rostock colleagues could testify to Schenk's ardent Nazi sympathies at the beginning of the regime. In 1934, Schenk joined the National Socialist Teachers Association, though he never officially joined the Nazi Party. In 1937, publishers of the official Hitler Youth publication *Die Musik* asked party officials in Rostock for an expert opinion on Schenk's political and ideological stance. Rostock's reply has been lost, but it was apparently an "extremely negative assessment" of Schenk, according to a later letter of clarification by *Die Musik* officials. Rostock had apparently complained about certain newspaper reviews Schenk had written that led to his removal as a musical correspondent. Yet the *Die Musik* officials—headed by the ardent Nazi editor Dr. Gerick—refused to accept a negative appraisal of Schenk's political reliability: "Our own experiences have mainly shown that Schenk has behaved as an impeccable National Socialist during his visits to Austria," they wrote in December 1937, several months before the Anschluss. "And in all matters of importance to cultural politics that required a personal confession of the individual representatives of the profession, Schenk has shown a clean and ideologically correct stance." There is no explanation for Rostock and Vienna's difference of opinion on Schenk. He showed his penchant for inserting Nazi ideology into his work in a book review he wrote for Gerick of A. Witeschnik's *The Strauss Dynasty* in November 1939. Schenk had lamented that the book did not clearly identify Jews, just as he would later complain that it was "repugnant" to write about a Jew like my grandfather.

In her study of German music, the scholar Pamela Potter has raised the possibility that Schenk's Nazi ideology and political connections had something to do with his appointment at the University of Vienna. It's a difficult theory to prove; Schenk's personnel file at the university is missing, along with several files on politically sensitive subjects. Left behind are only the notations "handed in by Prof. Erich Schenk" on empty folders. Potter wrote: "It is likely that Schenk, serving as Ordinarius after 1945, removed his documents after the war, perhaps to conceal his political involvement."

Schenk's political connections are clear in 1942, when he tried to arrange a project on the (alleged) Germanic roots of Gregorian chant with the Ahnenerbe Foundation, an SS organ that investigated "Aryan" cultural roots. His research proposals reached the ears of Heinrich Himmler, who favored the project. The Ahnenerbe Foundation also liked the idea but rejected Schenk's attempt to get one of his protegés assigned to head the research. Walter Wüst, the curator of the Ahnenerbe Foundation and an SS officer, apparently kept out of these discussions, soon put a stop to them. "I as representative of the German Academy have ended cooperation with Prof. Sch(enk). Why was I not consulted earlier?" he wrote on a letter from the foundation's secretary. The secretary indicated that Schenk had to be dealt with politely; he had friends in high places—connections that reached as high as Himmler.

Schenk was not only a Nazi collaborator, according to Ficker, but obviously an opportunist. In a post-war letter to the Education Ministry, Ficker wrote that many witnesses confirmed how Schenk "always proudly wore the party badge, but now claims he was never a member of the NSDAP. There is nothing that could better characterise his mindset: Because of his uncertainty about the future, he was too scared to openly and honestly join the party. But he still wore its emblem in order to appear a trustworthy follower to those party and state authorities who made decisions about his career."

This chameleon talent proved useful in his dealings with my Aunt Melanie and my grandfather's library. Once Melanie had rejected Schenk's offer of a visa to Italy in return for donating the library to the Musicology Seminar, he began planning an alternative way to get what he wanted. On March 31, 1941 he wrote a letter to the Reich's Ministry of Education regarding my grandfather's library:

A few weeks ago, the founder of the Music Seminar of Vienna, Guido Israel Adler, died. He left behind a well-known library that was initially secured by the Gestapo at the instigation of the leader of the lecturers association. And now there must be a decision about the fate of the library, i.e., if it should become the property of either the Music Seminar or the Vienna National Library, or if both these institutions should share the assets, respectively.

He went on to argue that the Musicology Seminar lacked many of the books in my grandfather's library, and thus should receive all its volumes. The letter is remarkable for several reasons: Schenk said the library already had been confiscated by the Gestapo, though that was not yet the case; he never mentioned that there was an heir, my Aunt Melanie, who had a legal right to the library even if she was a Jew; and he never raised the possibility of purchasing the library. The Education Ministry didn't consider these points either, but simply told Schenk that his university must indeed share my grandfather's library with the Vienna National Library. This gave Schenk the mandate for his future moves against my aunt.

Although Schenk had claimed the Musicology Seminar needed the books in my grandfather's library, Ficker in a post-war memo about the case begged to differ:

Since the library [of Guido Adler] consisted nearly totally of works which already were in possession of the library of the Seminar of Musicology, it was obvious that this request was not made primarily in the interest of the seminar, but rather in the interest of third persons. They had to recognize that here was a favorable opportunity to acquire cheaply those rejected duplicates of works that had long been unobtainable commercially.

Who the "third persons" were, Ficker did not say, nor did he have to. In his March 31 letter, Schenk neglected to mention a possible purchase of my grandfather's library, even though he later offered to buy a library left by a non-Jewish colleague. In 1942, Schenk asked the authorities for 3,000 Reichsmarks to purchase the library of deceased musicologist Joseph Zuth, whose specialty was guitar and lute music. Zuth's widow had offered to leave the estate to the University of Vienna free of charge, but Schenk wouldn't hear of it. The widow's financial situation was not good, he wrote to the authorities, and so some compensation for the library would be appropriate. It is telling how differently Schenk approached Jewish and non-Jewish property.

Although Melanie had declined Schenk's offer, she knew that the library was her only bargaining chip to safety. She turned again to Ficker, asking him to help her sell or trade Guido's library in exchange for safe passage to Munich and the right to live there in peace. Ficker approached the Munich City Library and received a favorable reply for an unusual reason: My aunt was the niece of Professor Ernst Berger, who died in a hostage murder in Munich in 1919. He was killed during a fight between right-wing precursors of the Nazis and the communists. The Nazis later celebrated the dead, including Berger, as first martyrs of the Nazi cause.

Melanie's connection to Berger opened doors. As Ficker wrote in a letter to the Austrian authorities after the war, "They [Munich City Library officials] not only offered Ms. Adler the protection we had asked for, but they offered to pay her a fair price for the library despite the fact that it was Jewish property." If it hadn't been for Schenk and Heiserer, my aunt might have sold the library to Munich, received a letter of protection that kept her from deportation, and lived through the war in the company of Ficker's family in Munich. But it was not to be.

Chapter Eight

THE BETRAYAL

E ven after Melanie rejected Schenk's offer, Heiserer continued to consult with him behind the scenes. In a letter to Schenk on April 4, 1941, Heiserer mentioned "meetings with professors Haas and Nowak,"—both colleagues of Schenk. Heiserer continued: "In accordance with our agreement the official inventory of Dr. Adler's estate . . . will be carried out on June 9, 1941." Whether the agreement mentioned in the letter was between Heiserer and Schenk or Heiserer and professors Haas and Nowak, the result was the same—Melanie's attorney worked to get the library into the hands of Schenk's Musicology Seminar, against the wishes of his client. As Heiserer kept Schenk and his colleagues abreast of the Adler probate proceedings, he obstructed the Munich City Library plan. On April 9, 1941 Rudolf von Ficker sent a letter to Heiserer regarding that arrangement:

To Dr. Heiserer, Attorney, Vienna I, Opernring 1

According to information given to me by (Miss) Dr. M. Adler in

Vienna, the library of her recently deceased father is supposed to
be sold. I am therefore free to inform you that the Munich City
Library is seriously considering purchasing the library and has
requested me to obtain further information in that regard. As
the administrator of the estate, I hereby inform you of that and
ask you to please give me at the appropriate time further
information about the possibilities for such an acquisition of
the library. Above all, it would be most desirable to look into the
catalogue.

Rudolf v. Ficker m.p.

Heiserer never answered the letter. Instead, Ficker received
an alarming letter from Melanie on May 4 revealing the trap
that would slowly close around her. There was to be an official
inventory of the library in June, as Heiserer had informed
Schenk, but Schenk's colleagues wanted an earlier look at the
goods. Heiserer acquired the keys to the library at Lannerstrasse
9, and told Melanie of the consequences if she refused to allow
the inventory—arrest by the Gestapo. Melanie wrote to Ficker:

My letter may hardly be in your hands by now and here is already my
second one. The reason for that is that they want to put pressure on me.
On Tuesday, as I mentioned, the matter (library) is supposed to be
inspected. Most likely by Sch(enk) and N(owak), already known to you
as being interested in it. The attorney is no help to me, as you can see by
the fact that up to now he couldn't be bothered to reply to you. The
inspection on Tuesday has been forced on me by the attorney who in my
absence obtained the key to the library. He is threatening me with the
Gestapo in order to intimidate me and to play into the hands of the
other ones.

After an impromptu examination of the library two days
later on May 6, Melanie sat and wrote yet another letter to
Ficker. Nowak and Haas had conducted the inspection, not
Schenk. Heiserer had told Melanie that he didn't know the

professors' names, yet the three men arrived at Melanie's home together. "This circumstance, though seemingly a trifle, tells me enough," Melanie wrote. The men pored through the entire library, at times looking for specific items. Haas wanted to find an autographed Beethoven manuscript. My aunt watched, helpless, but finally had the courage to ask: "What is the true intention of you gentleman?" In her letter, she didn't mention who made the reply. One of the men said, "This (library) has to remain in Vienna, according to the intention of the deceased." Heiserer then spoke up. "It is Jewish property, and I already have said that there is also another offer in existence." Nowak and Haas, as my aunt wrote, did not reply. Heiserer did not pursue the point. Melanie clearly saw that "the attorney sided with them." She continued:

I already wrote to you that this man is putting pressure on me with his claim that the Gestapo has confiscated the library. Yesterday, I had a conversation with somebody who is familiar with the ways of the police. He shares the opinion that this has only been said to me to intimidate me and to deprive me of my freedom to move and make decisions. That is of great advantage for all involved except for myself.

On May 14—the day before Germany's blitzkrieg reached the Netherlands—the district court stated that Heiserer had been given power of attorney by Melanie and my father Achim. This was not only unlikely, but impossible. My father was living in the United States at the time and had been for nearly three years. Besides the fact that little mail got through between the United States and Austria at that time, my father would have had no incentive to sign over power of attorney to a Nazi lawyer. The probate files in Vienna contain no document to prove this ever happened. It is far more likely that the Nazis or the court assigned Heiserer to shepherd the probate through the court, ensuring that all of my grandfather's assets ended in the coffers of the Reich. Given conditions in Austria, Heiserer had a month to furnish the court with a declaration of inheritance, and to give the imperial medals of honor that my grandfather had earned to the mint in Vienna where they would be melted down to help fund the Reich's war effort. The court accepted Melanie's right to inherit as Guido's heir on May 27, 1941. A day later, the German war machine pounded Belgium.

The Munich City Library deal was not yet dead. The library contacted Heiserer directly on May 30, asking that Guido's collection be indexed and appraised in preparation for the sale. Again, there is no record of Heiserer replying. Melanie told Ficker in a letter from around the same time that "the City Library has contacted the attorney. He is becoming increasingly impertinent." In Vienna, an official appraisal of the library was made on June 9 by the court-appointed appraiser Carl Borufka and the antiquarian Christian Nebehay. They declared that the collection of books, music manuscripts and 20 paper containers full of letters from renowned men like Brahms and Bruckner should be kept together, and they valued it at 13,185 Reichsmarks (about $52,740 in present U.S. dollars)—well below market price, no doubt because of the library's Jewish owner and the unique market conditions during the war. The actual inventory by Nebehay and Borufka is missing, and it is unknown if it contained some of the library's most precious items, including a death mask of Beethoven and the Mahler manuscript of "Ich bin der Welt abhanden gekommen."

In view of Potter's statement that Schenk purged his files of any involvement with the Nazis, he may have disposed of the inventory of the library when accused of wrongdoing after the war. In all likelihood, the inventory listed the items which were looted when Heiserer had full access to my grandfather's house, library and safe. Since it should have been part of the probate court files in Vienna, the fact that it is missing points to the possibility that Heiserer had a hand in this also. Three days later, my Aunt Melanie fired Heiserer. In a June letter to Ficker, she wrote that the probate hearing related to the library had already taken place. "But this was still done under Dr. H[eiserer]," she wrote.

On June 27, Heiserer informed the Musicology Seminar that: "In reference to my telephone conversation with Prof. Schenk, I permit myself to repeat information which was given to me by Dr. Melanie Sarah Adler, the heiress of Dr. Guido Isr[ael] Adler. In a letter of June 12 of this year, she terminated my power of attorney to act on her behalf in the above probate proceeding." Melanie had appointed Dr. Johann Kellner of Vienna I, Babenbergerstrasse 1, as Heiserer's replacement. In his letter to the Musicology Seminar, Heiserer also mentioned that he would inform the Gestapo of Melanie's decision, "insofar as they [the Gestapo] entrusted me with the safekeeping of the library after the preliminary confiscation order by my acceptance of the keys to the rooms of the library. I was also entrusted with the obligation to ensure that a sale of the library can only take place with the consent of the State Police. I have to be dependent on the opinion of the Secret State Police Central Office in Vienna whether/or to what extent I can subsequently carry out this function." Heiserer enclosed a copy, now also missing, of the official inventory and appraisal of my grandfather's library.

Schenk replied the next day that he wanted to make a legal claim on behalf of the "Society for Musicology of the Eastern Marches" to one of my grandfather's complete 83-volume *Monuments of Music in Austria*—which was almost impossible to find on the market, and extremely expensive (estimated at 2,000 Reichsmarks) if it could be found for sale. Guido had possessed a complete and a partial-bound series, one on handmade paper. He had told Ficker many times that Melanie and Achim should each inherit one copy. Schenk claimed a copy of the series for the Society for Musicology though he already had a copy of his own. Heiserer had told Melanie in April or early May that one copy of the series belonging to Guido was given free of cost to the *Monuments'* current editor, who at that time happened to be Schenk. In a post-war letter, Ficker wrote: "Thus from the very beginning he [Schenk] abused Ms. Adler's precarious situation by making a completely unjustified claim to the library in order to secure for himself free of charge what is arguably its most precious item."

Soon after my Aunt Melanie fired Heiserer, the German Army defeated France and Hitler celebrated a triumph on the streets of Paris. The Third Reich would have looked invincible if not for its failure to break through English air power to invade Britain. On June 22, Hitler turned his panzers on the Soviet Union. At about the same time in Vienna, Melanie wrote Ficker an update on the Nazi attempt to evict her from her home on Lannerstrasse 9. The authorities had set a date for eviction: August 15. Melanie's new attorney, Johann Kellner, appeared to have better success than Heiserer in advocating on Melanie's behalf. Melanie had written to Ficker about the change of attorneys. "The first success of this is that I am allowed to remain in the flat," she commented.

This must have been a great consolation to my aunt, considering that most of the Jews remaining in Austria had been herded into the new Vienna ghetto. Though still at home, she had made it clear to Ficker that she intended to leave Austria now that her father was dead. Only in Italy, or perhaps Munich, could Melanie hope to outlive the Nazis. That may speak to the closeness she felt for her Italian relatives. More than half a century before the Anschluss, Guido's oldest brother Robert had emigrated with his wife to Milan, where his four children and six grandchildren were born. Guido's widowed sister Clementine Eisenschitz had followed Robert to Milan in 1885 with two of her children. Her daughter married an Italian war hero, General Francisco Rocca, and Guido was close to both the Adler and Rocca families. It is unlikely that Robert or Clementine, Melanie's uncle and aunt, were alive when she tried to flee to Italy. Their children and grandchildren were, however, still in Milan. After Guido's death, Melanie had never mentioned the possibility of joining my family in the United

States. It may have been impossible for her to get a second visa
to the United States, since her first had expired in 1938.

Melanie was in a quandary. She knew she must leave Austria
soon, yet she had to complete the probate proceedings in order
to get the inheritance she needed to pay the emigration tax
levied by the Nazis, and to bargain for an exit visa or letter of
protection. Going underground in these early months after
Guido's death was not an option, and neither was fleeing
secretly over the border into Switzerland or Italy. Besides,
Melanie had other priorities than flight: Schenk had offered
her an exit visa in exchange for her father's library, but she
had refused in fear that the books and manuscripts would be
scattered and impossible to find after the war. Had she worried
only about her own safety, she would have jumped at Schenk's
offer and joined her family in Italy. Jews were not safe in
Mussolini's realm either, but at least Melanie would have been
outside of the German Reich. As it was, she chose to keep the
library together, even at the risk that no better offer for a trade
would come in time to save her from deportation. And the
Munich City Library gave her some hope that her gamble was
worth it.

Like most Jews in Austria in the war years, my Aunt Melanie
lived in a shrunken world. There was no work for Jews, and
Jewish grocery stores, clothing shops, tailors and other small
retail businesses had closed their doors because of Nazi boycotts
and demands to liquidate all Jewish assets. Most parks and
theaters were closed to Jews. Even a walk in the street after
hours could be a hazard if Melanie had been recognized as a
Jew, or if the police had demanded her identification card
stamped with the "J" for *Jud.* She had been forced to take on
the middle name "Sara," another Nazi identifier of her
Jewishness, just as all Jewish men with "Aryan" names had to
take on the middle name "Israel." Finally, there was always the
fear that a Gestapo fist would be the next to pound on the
door. "I haven't had an hour's peace in weeks, and I can't go
on any longer," Melanie wrote to Ficker on July 7, 1941.

In these last days, I have been summoned three times by the Gestapo, and today I was berated ferociously by three officials after an interrogation that lasted two hours. The reason for that was that I did not want to sign the record of the interrogation, which I had been expressly forbidden to do by my attorney. But I collapsed, because all of this got to be too much for me and I finally signed . . . The main thing is the library and we know very well who is behind all that.

At last, the Gestapo had reached my aunt, just as Richard Heiserer had predicted. "I am totally confused and don't know if I can give you a clear view because of the chaos that surrounds me," she wrote to Ficker.

Heiserer still had full access to my grandfather's library, which gave him more than enough opportunity to take any items that interested him, including the Mahler manuscript. Though Heiserer was no longer Melanie's attorney, he still carried the keys to the Adler library, and still answered to the Gestapo in matters related to the library. He could enter it whenever he wished, without Melanie's permission. And Melanie couldn't get in at all without Heiserer. Ficker noted in a post-war letter that "after every library visit, Dr. Heiserer took the keys to the room and thus even Mel[i] couldn't get in anymore." Heiserer had many chances to comb through the books and manuscripts at his leisure, with no witnesses. The safe where my grandfather had stored the Mahler manuscript would have been opened for the recent inventories, and Heiserer no doubt saw the signed Mahler there. The fact that this manuscript by a well-known composer sat in a safe at all was a clue to Heiserer of its potential value. The musical score, slipped into a folio folder, could have been spirited from the house with ease. Decades later, Heiserer's son would claim that his father acquired the Mahler manuscript as payment for legal services, possibly before Guido died, despite the absence of any records to connect Heiserer to the Adler family before his death.

After Guido's death, Heiserer, in conjunction with the Gestapo, worked to curtail any financial independence Melanie might have had. In 1947, Ficker learned from Egon Wellesz that Melanie had borrowed money from an Adler family friend he called Mrs. Prochaska—probably Margarete Prohaska, wife of the composer Karl Prohaska. The daughter of the painter Julius Schmid, Margarete, probably knew Melanie when they were children. In 1889, the Adler and Schmid families had spent their vacation together in St. Gilgen/Wolfgangsee, a fashionable stop in Upper Austria. Margarete Prohaska knew Heiserer, and even testified at his denazification proceedings after the war. She was also a warm supporter of Schenk. It is even possible that she had brought Heiserer to Melanie and lent her money to enlist his services. The women had once been friends, but Melanie later changed her feelings. She "suspected that the attorney Dr. Heiserer's hostile attitude could be traced back to her [Mrs. Prohaska]," Ficker wrote. "Even though Melanie never mentioned having money problems, it still makes sense that due to the closing of all her savings accounts, she was forced to borrow money. She couldn't pay back the money because on the demand of Dr. Heiserer, a friend of Mrs. Proch[aska], the Gestapo had blocked her inheritance." Needless to add, Heiserer's impoverishment of Melanie in favor of the Reich was in direct conflict with his duties as her lawyer.

Heiserer's duty as he saw it was to ensure that all of the assets in my grandfather's estate were seized for the benefit of the Reich. But how was he to be paid? It is possible that Melanie did so with money from her account or from money borrowed from Prohaska. But given her efforts to preserve her father's entire library, even at the risk of personal harm, it is inconceivable that she would have given Heiserer the one item that her father valued enough to keep in a safe—the Mahler manuscript. What is far more likely is that Heiserer's "specialty" of representing Jews with assets was born from the knowledge that he would have access to their homes and valuables. He would be free-to take stock of the items and appropriate whatever he cared to without fear of detection or consequences.

Heiserer's son would claim 60 years later that his father had acquired the Mahler as a legal fee, but this is nothing more than an attempt to revise the history of Nazi Austria. Besides, if Heiserer had accepted the manuscript as a fee for his very limited legal services, he would not have put in a claim against Melanie's estate after the war. Yet he did. A letter written by an official of the Regional Tax Authority in Vienna on June 7th, 1945 discussed the confiscation of the estate: "Some attorneys, including Dr. Heiserer, have put claims against the confiscated assets." That claim strongly suggests that he wasn't paid at all— either with the Mahler manuscript or with money. My father's post-war attorney and the Tax Office did not clear up these claims because "the legal situation was somewhat muddled," and "none of the interested persons seemed to care about it any longer." Did Heiserer finally decide that his Gestapo-aided "appropriation" of the Mahler would suffice? Or did he drop his claim out of fear that an official investigation into Melanie's assets would reveal his role in the confiscation?

Because of Heiserer's questionable ethics, he may not have believed himself guilty of any misdeeds, especially after the war had ended. Like Schenk, he had used the anti-Jewish laws of the time to enrich himself. And given the cast of participants in the affair of the Adler library—Schenk, Orel, Nowak, Nebehay, Borufka, Haas and others—Heiserer may have convinced himself that his was only a small part of the proceedings. This would have been simple, since most efforts to "Aryanize" property in Nazi Austria were coordinated so that no single person could be accused of having committed the deed. As a recent study of Vienna's "Aryanization" years noted: "Complicity was of high importance: The more people who were involved, the easier it was to shuffle off any personal responsibility onto the group . . . . The offenders created an aura of bogus legality." Heiserer operated in an environment

in which "corruption and greed constituted the driving forces
behind an absurd façade of normalcy."

On August 5, 1941, the Nazis radically changed their policy
about the emigration of Jews. Those between the ages of 18
and 45 were forbidden to leave the Reich. As the war continued
the Nazis gave up their goal of a land free of Jews; cheap Jewish
labor in Reich factories was more important. The emigration
ban didn't affect Melanie, who was 53 years old, but the news
must have unsettled her. How long would it be before the Nazis
banned Jewish emigration altogether? Time was running out.
The Gestapo continued to harass Melanie. On August 6
she wrote to Ficker: "Two days ago the attorney spent a whole
morning at the Gestapo, as he told me. They want to get the
library for free and also the flat. The attorney declared that he
will not give away either one." The support of my aunt's new
lawyer Kellner differed vastly from Heiserer's threats of the
Gestapo. "But surely the Gestapo will want to take revenge on
me," Melanie continued to Ficker. "They supposedly said to
the attorney: 'There is still enough room in Poland.' I don't
trust any of this, since I have become their focal point because
of the library." Melanie finished the letter with a mention of
her only clear offer of help so far, from the Munich City Library:
"I want to handle the matter of the library as obligingly as
possible for Munich, and I'll ask them to give me a written
assurance that I may travel in peace to Munich as often as I
want."

Melanie had written to the city library in July asking for an
update. On August 1, she received a reply that the library had
tried to contact Heiserer two months before, apparently to no
avail. "We are interested in literature on musicology, but can
only begin further negotiations when we are informed of the
size, content and price of the library," a library official wrote.
Melanie told Ficker in an August 8 letter that she wanted the
library packed up and shipped to Munich, an appraisal done
at her expense and an index of the books made if one could

not be found. "After that, you may make a proposal to the city, or if this does not suit you, I will do it myself. I am convinced that the city will then be satisfied and will buy the library. All of this is done out of consideration that from here the right thing will never and under no circumstances be done for me." Unfortunately, Melanie was locked out of the library, since the keys remained in Heiserer's hands. By mid-September, none of her plans to prepare the library for Munich had been carried out.

After the war, Ficker summed up the failure of the Munich library purchase: "Munich didn't make any offer at all. It wasn't able to make an offer because the three existing copies of the library catalogue had disappeared after Adler's death . . . Dr. Heiserer ignored a request for information from Munich, and afterward the Gestapo was used to seize the library and to prosecute its heir." It could not have been coincidence that all three copies of the library catalogue had disappeared. Heiserer had forwarded one copy to Schenk, who later showed a penchant for concealing incriminating evidence by hiding or destroying his university personnel files. He could have easily spirited away his copy; Heiserer's was also conveniently lost. There must have been a concerted effort to destroy any records which may have been used to prove the extent of the looting that took place. Melanie had only one last hope. It lay in the most unlikely of places: Hitler's beloved festival city of Bayreuth, which was ruled by the composer Richard Wagner's daughter-in-law, Winifred.

Chapter Nine

THE LAST HOPE

Winifred Marjorie Williams was born in Hastings, England on June 23, 1897, and lost both her parents by the age of two. As a child, she moved to Berlin to the home of the pianist Karl Klindworth, a distant relative and an old friend of Richard Wagner. Young Winifred was introduced to *Parsifal, Lohengrin* and Wagner's other famous works, as well as an antisemitism that was a part of the Klindworth household. In 1914, she attended six evenings of Wagner music at the annual music festival in the *Festspielhaus* in Bayreuth. The 17-year-old was a stately young woman with a straight-nosed profile and blue eyes that drew the attention of Siegfried Wagner— Richard and Cosima Wagner's only son. Siegfried, 28 years older than Winifred, married her in 1915. The bride became a German citizen.

Siegfried, who composed music and directed opera performances, left the organization of the Bayreuth performances largely in the hands of his energetic young wife. In 1923, Winifred met Adolf Hitler for the first time and became devoted to the rising young politician and his vision for a new Germany. After the Munich *putsch* later in the year, Winifred sent letters and packages full of blankets, jackets, socks, food and books to Hitler in his jail at the Fortress Landsberg. For Christmas, Winifred organized a gift collection for Hitler, and sent him one of the presents he most requested—paper, which he would use to write *Mein Kampf.* Winifred's husband and mother-in-law both died in 1930, leaving 30-year-old Winifred the mistress of Bayreuth. She supported Hitler's rise to chancellor in 1933. "Wolf" and "Winnie," as they called each other, had grown so close that Hitler treated Winifred's children like his own, and there were whispers of a marriage. Winifred believed Hitler would reawaken Germans to the romantic ideals of knightly heroism, strength, duty and loyalty that would lead the country to glory. Hitler would, as Winifred wrote, "pull the sword out of the German oak," a reference to Richard Wagner's *Ring of the Nibelungen.*

During the war, Winifred did not have to worry about the financial situation of the Wagner festivals. Hitler exempted the Bayreuth theater from taxes and subsidized it out of the Reich's coffers. Soon the Bayreuth Festival with its marathon performances of Wagner music became an annual Nazi pilgrimage. The festival's popularity with Hitler and the Nazis stemmed from Wagner's own vision of Germanic greatness: His operas colored the German past with supernatural beings, goddesses of death, fearless heroes, maidens who killed themselves out of love and loyalty to the hero. Such tales reached into the imaginations of Germans, and the Nazi Party used the images to weave its own myths. In charge of Bayreuth, Winifred Wagner thus had an immense influence on Hitler and the Nazi Party.

Winifred joined the Party in 1927, evidence of her early passion for the National Socialists. But even within that seemingly monolithic party, she demonstrated a mind of her own that irritated more hard-nosed Nazis. Winifred was appalled at the violent excesses of the party in the 1930s and 1940s, and was not afraid to tell Hitler what she thought. She told him it was scandalous that hardworking Jewish Festspielhaus workers were spat upon in public, and she refused to fire leftists from her staff simply because of political opinion. "Where I can prevent an act of violence by the party, I will put forth my passionate opposition," she said. Nor did she see this attitude as contrary to her devotion for Hitler. She suspected that the Führer didn't know of the most brutal elements of Nazi Germany; his awareness of what happened during the war was addled, she thought, by slow, poisonous injections from Hitler's doctor Theodor Morell.

Artists, Jews and homosexuals threatened by the Gestapo began to flock to Winifred for help—successfully. Relatives of the novelist Thomas Mann fled to Switzerland with her assistance, and the Jewish conductor Paul Ottenheimer was saved from Auschwitz in 1943 (though he was deported to Theresienstadt two years later). The elderly writer Elsa Bernstein, who wrote the libretto for Engelbert Humperdinck's opera *Königskinder*, received an exit visa for the U.S. with Winifred's help, but didn't use it when Winifred was unable to secure one for Elsa's sister. Elsa outlived the war because of Winifred's influence; she was allowed to live in the "prominent camp" of Theresienstadt, where prisoners received better food, clean beds and visitors. Winifred's guardian angel reputation grew until about 75 percent of the letters she received during the war were cries for help—some 20 letters a day.

After Melanie came under the heel of the Gestapo and was threatened with eviction herself, she sent a letter to Winifred, but received no answer. In a letter to Ficker on July 7, 1941, Melanie wrote: "It's high time that something has to happen by Mrs. W(agner) in order for me to get some peace." On July 21, Ficker appealed to the German State Music Conductor B. Wetzelberger in Munich to contact Winifred on Melanie's behalf. Ficker enclosed a copy of one of Melanie's letters, and explained to Wetzelberger the background of the case. He informed him that Robert Haas of the National Library in Vienna, Schenk, Nowak, a former assistant of my grandfather, combined to harass Melanie:

From these three gentlemen . . . stem all that harassment against the daughter. I therefore would like to ask you to achieve some relief for the daughter by your intercession with Mrs. Winifred Wagner . . . May I ask you to describe the facts from there [Munich] and to arrange that the daughter does not experience any more difficulties from the Viennese Gestapo because of this library matter?

In late August, Melanie derived some hope from Winifred's reply:

Unfortunately, your letter was forwarded to me only today . . . I also found a letter here from Mr. Wetzelsberger, which contained various illuminating attachments. Now, of course, I do not know if the ominous August 15 really has brought you the eviction from your flat or not. I hope this is not the case. After carefully considering the matter, I have forwarded it to Vice Mayor Blaschke in Vienna.

Melanie was still in her home on September 15, the day the Nazis decreed that every Jew over age 6 must wear the Star of David. She remained at Lannerstrasse 9, probably in hiding, perhaps in the attic, as was indicated in a later letter. On August 18, a letter from a Jewish attorney about her JUVA tax obligation had been delivered to Wipplingerstrasse 24 in Vienna's district I. Melanie may have forwarded her mail there for pickup to keep up the fiction that she had really left Lannerstrasse 9.

In September, Melanie's case passed out of the hands of the Viennese vice mayor to the chief of the Gestapo in Munich. In a September 15 letter to Ficker, Melanie mentioned that the library had been closed by the Gestapo. But she still clung to the hope that something would come out of the plan to sell her father's library to the Munich City Library:

I have come to the opinion that an initiative from the outside is needed in order to free me from here. The matter of the library could be such an initiative. But if I am not in a position to offer an index of contents and make a purchase offer to the Munich City Library, this matter will never begin to move forward at all, because the city administration rightfully demands a base for negotiations. What am I to do? I live in enough fear and worry and so far this really well-meaning letter from Mrs. Wagner has achieved exactly nothing.

Meanwhile, the Nazis moved forward to confiscate the assets of my immediate family, though we had been in the United States for three years. On September 26, the Vienna Gestapo declared that "all of the personal property and personal assets, including real estate holdings, as well as all rights and claims of: Dr. Adler Hubert Joachim Israel [*sic*] . . . and that of his wife Marianne maiden name Fischmann . . . as well as that of their children Evelyne Ruth . . . and that of Thomas Carl . . . all last residing at Vienna I, Gonzagagasse 5, and possessing German citizenship are confiscated in favor of the German Reich. The basis is public security and order." With that order, my father lost to the Nazis his part ownership in the houses on Gonzagagasse and Lannerstrasse. The Gestapo made clear that "No right of appeal against this confiscation order is permitted." My father would have to wait until after the war to reclaim what he could.

In October, the Nazis began a large-scale, systematic deportation of Jews out of Vienna. Melanie's fear for her life grew as she wrote to Ficker early in the month:

The deportations to Poland begin again. On the 15th of this month the first transports will leave. Five thousand people from Vienna. Because of the matter of the library I am widely known enough already, and because of it there exists a case file on me. So, I'll be perhaps on their list . . . I ask you most urgently to make it possible for me to speak with Mr. W[agner] . . . The best thing would be a letter of protection. Such letters are frequently used.

When nothing had happened by late October, my Aunt Melanie sent another letter to Ficker:

"I now know definitely that Professor E[rich] Sch[enk] has secured the library for himself."

Yet Melanie made one last attempt to foil Schenk's plans. On October 26, 1941 she appealed once again to Winifred Wagner:

> *Most revered, merciful lady,*
>
> *My long silence looks like ungratefulness.*
>
> *In reality, a time of varying experiences in my life lies behind me. What on one day was taken as the full truth was already wiped out the next day. An anxiety has hit me from a side I had no suspicion of. Because of that, I could never get at a clear picture.*
>
> *The fact is that for now, I am still in my home. But after my most recent experiences, I no longer know how long this will be the case and what my fate will be since it isn't known if your intercession on my behalf has been a success. What remains is only my large, large gratitude and reverence for you, honorable and merciful lady!*
>
> *And this is also the main motivation behind the request I am about to make. Its fulfilment would have been in my father's interest and for myself, it would mean high honor.*
>
> *My father left behind a voluminous library of music history. He spent his entire life assembling it, and I know from experts that it is truly good. For these reasons I would like to offer the library to the House Wahnfried—the one temple of the muses which made a deep everlasting impression on my father.*
>
> *If you, very revered lady, do not want to place the library in*

Wahnfried, then I kindly ask you to accept it for any non-commercial public purpose you consider appropriate.

And now I come to the part of my writing that is the most difficult for me, because I want to ask something for myself and because my entire future depends on the fulfilment of my request. And that is the securing of a letter of protection that would finally secure some peace for me, my possessions and my work.

Now I am finished, though I don't know if I have managed to express everything as it truly is. For this reason I take the liberty to repeat my plea if you very revered lady would kindly deign to grant me an audience.

Yours thankfully devoted,

Dr. Melanie Adler
Wien XIX, Lannerstraße 9
Daughter of the musicologist and university Professor Adler (Guido) in Vienna.

By the time Melanie received a response from Winifred, a terrible blow had fallen on all of the Jews remaining in the Third Reich. On November 10, 1941, the Nazis banned all Jewish emigration. The borders closed, and the only transport remaining for Jews was the infamous deportation train. "This is what it is like now," Melanie wrote Ficker on November 11. "Suddenly somebody is taken from one's flat and then not left alone anymore . . . Then one is locked into a cattle car and then transported to Poland . . . Mrs. Wagner, of course, does not have any knowledge of all that and she is thinking there would be enough time for everything." Melanie sounded morbid and depressed in her letter. Perhaps the isolation of living in hiding had taken its toll, or perhaps she was simply frustrated at the naiveté of Winifred Wagner. The mistress of Bayreuth appeared to have no idea of how dangerous my aunt's situation was. In her letter to Ficker, Melanie enclosed a copy of Winifred's response to her appeal to secure the library at Wahnfried, the Wagner family villa:

I have thought over again and again how to help you—but I cannot see any possibility to effect the letter of protection for you which you requested. But on the other hand, I do not see any danger in your remaining in Vienna, since you have been left in peace so far—so to speak—in your house and since you should move to the attic anyway. Anyway, of course, I would be prepared to create a secure and decent place for the valuable library of your father and I also would . . . have room for several thousand volumes, but I would hate to deprive you of this treasure. And on the other hand I hardly would be in a position to offer you any adequate financial remuneration for it. But if you could inform me about its estimated value, it could be considered, of course, to buy the library in installments from you.

Melanie would hardly have called the months of Gestapo interrogations peaceful, and if she had indeed moved into the attic of Lannerstrasse 9, it was certainly not her own choice to do so. Given the situation in Vienna, selling her father's library in installments must have sounded almost ludicrous. Winifred assumed my aunt lived in a world in which Melanie controlled her possessions, and could count on a future. Instead, Melanie lived day to day, hour by hour, hidden in her own home. She did not pick up her letters, did not appear when Nazi authorities called her, and did not respond when they ordered her to return one of her father's remaining gold medals. Karola Fischmann, a great cousin of my aunt, would later testify that Melanie "lived in hiding and that people took care of her."

The only way to convince Winifred of the need for speed was to visit her in person. Melanie arrived in Bayreuth at midday on December 9. As she wrote to Ficker later:

I was received most warmly . . . (I) told her of my request and saw her earnest will to help me. She also assured me that my cause was not that

*difficult and that she would be able to do something. Before her arrival
in Vienna, though, I should inquire which persons needed to be
approached. She would then influence them favorably toward her, and
after that would continue to work for me in Berlin . . . and then try to
bring everything to a favorable conclusion.*

On December 11, after the Japanese had attacked U.S.
warships at Pearl Harbor, Hitler declared war on the United
States. Perhaps it was welcome news to Melanie that this large
new enemy of the Reich had entered the war. In any event,
her last letters to Rudolf von Ficker were more optimistic than
her situation warranted. Her hopes were tied up in Winifred
Wagner. Melanie told Ficker sometime in December that
Winifred "had taken the matter of protection firmly in hand,
so that a positive outcome can be counted on."

Her last known letter to Ficker arrived at the end of 1941:
"In the meantime, I have turned personally to Mrs. W," Melanie
wrote on a Sunday in December. "She now knows everything
and reacted with a telegram and I now hope that something
will be done on my behalf. Something for me. That is now
more necessary than ever. The library, of course, belongs to
Mrs. Wagner."

Despite my aunt's conviction, any help from Winifred
Wagner would come too late. Around Christmas 1941, Melanie
fled from the house on Lannerstrasse 9. It is not known exactly
what happened that made her finally leave the confinement
of the attic, and no one knows where she lived afterward. At
some point, Winifred Wagner gave up working to secure the
Adler library for House Wahnfried. "Of course, this plan could
not be carried out because the city of Vienna had learned about
the plan and because it claimed the library for itself," Winifred
noted in her defense during her post-war denazification
process.

Rudolf von Ficker never heard from Melanie again. In

March 1942, he wrote her a letter but did not receive a response. Curious about what happened, he travelled from Munich to Vienna and arrived at the Musicology Seminar at the University of Vienna on May 8. Coincidentally, Professor Erich Schenk himself, whom Ficker had never met before, happened to be directing the unloading of documents and books from my grandfather's library. Schenk seemed perfectly happy to tell Ficker what had happened: Melanie had refused the offer of a visa to Italy in exchange for the library, and Schenk therefore "had no choice but to let the Gestapo confiscate the library," as Ficker wrote in a post-war letter to the Ministry of Education. Schenk did try to shuffle off responsibility for the confiscation by telling Ficker the whole business had been suggested to him "from above," which Ficker took to be the university's powerful College of Lecturers. Schenk would later reap his rewards for "saving" the valuable Adler library for the university.

Schenk also knew that Melanie's continued refusal to hand over the library to the Gestapo had sealed her fate: Schenk had called this behavior of my aunt "*saudumm*," or "stupid beyond belief," Ficker wrote. The result of that—"Off to Poland!" as Schenk said to Ficker. "From Prof. Schenk's own words it is evident that there was a clear connection between the persecution of Ms. Adler and her displacement to Poland on the one hand, and his plans for the library on the other."

At the time, neither Schenk nor Ficker knew that Melanie had not been sent to Poland. Understandably, they assumed her life would end there, since some of the most notorious concentration camps, including Treblinka and Auschwitz, were in Poland. Jews had been transported to former Polish territory from all of the lands then controlled by the German Reich. But Poland was not the scene of Melanie's last days. Probably in May 1942, her hiding place was betrayed, and she finally fell into the hands of the Gestapo. The head of the security police, Reinhard Heydrich, had earlier ordered that some Jews from

the west be transported to Minsk (in today's Belarus) and killed
immediately upon arrival. On May 6, the first deportation train
to Minsk left Vienna's Aspang station with 998 Jews aboard.
Melanie's turn came on May 20, when she boarded transport
number 22 for Minsk. On June 2, my grandmother Ida
Fischmann entered transport 24. What then happened to my
family at the end of the train ride, after days of claustrophobia,
filth, hunger and terror, can be reconstructed with the help
of the Jewish Archives in Vienna and eyewitness testimony.

Between May and October 1942, more than 15,000 people
arrived in Minsk from Cologne, Vienna, the Theresienstadt
ghetto in Austria, and Königsberg in East Prussia. Melanie's
train probably stopped at the freight station in Minsk sometime
between 4 and 7 in the morning, early enough for the weary,
terrified passengers to be unloaded before the population of
Minsk awakened. Melanie and the other people in transport
22 were herded into an assembly hall, where the secret police
took their money and luggage. Then the selection began. The
police strolled through the crowd of deportees looking for a
few strong people to work as slaves in the Maly Trostinec camp,
a former Soviet collective farm. Only 20 to 50 people were
chosen from a transport that may have contained 1,000 people
or more. The thin, 54-year-old Melanie would never have been
considered for hard labor.

A survivor of one of the transports wrote later about his
stopover in Minsk in early May 1942:

*For the transport of the sick, of persons who went out of their mind during
the journey, the aged and infirm (about 200 in number in our transport)
boxcars stood waiting—great, gray, closed motor-vans—into which the
people were thrown one on top of the other in confusion . . .*

These were likely the gas vans, known as "Death Vans" by
civilians, in which exhaust fumes pumped into the body of the
van killed everyone inside. Two such vans were stationed
Minsk in early 1942. Each could hold about 50 to 60 victims. S

officer Dr. August Becker, who oversaw the use of gas vans in the former Soviet territories, coolly observed in an official memo that the gas van executions were not carried out properly in his jurisdiction:

In order to get the Aktion finished as quickly as possible the driver presses down on the accelerator as far as it will go. As a result the persons to be executed die of suffocation and do not doze off as was planned. It has proved that if my instructions are followed and the levers are properly adjusted death comes faster and the prisoners fall asleep peacefully. Distorted faces and excretions, such as were observed before, no longer occur.

Assuming that my Aunt Melanie had survived the transport journey physically and mentally, she would have been spared from the monstrous gas van. Instead, she joined the hundreds of others who were crammed into trucks and driven about 18 kilometers out of the city to a lonely pine wood outside of Maly Trostinec. Under order of the SS, trenches about 3 meters deep and 50 meters high had already been dug when Melanie and the others arrived. The terror that must have seized the deportees when they first caught sight of the trenches and of the 20 or more SS marksmen stationed at the edges, is unimaginable. The shooting began almost immediately. It went on so long that the marksmen had to be replaced by fresh troops, who later were themselves replaced, over and over until the transport trucks were empty.

It is doubtful that any remains of my Aunt Melanie can be found. In 1943, the German army was battered by the Soviets, and the SS began covering up any evidence of mass murder in advance of a German retreat. The SS forced Soviet POWs to dig up the half-rotten corpses outside Maly Trostinec and burn them on railroad tracks. Of the 9,000 Austrian Jews deported to Maly Trostinec, only 17 survived.

Chapter Ten

FICKER'S MISSION

In 1945, it was the Soviets who reached Austria first. The Red Army rolled into Vienna and set up a provisional government that on April 27 re-established the independence of Austria from Germany. Hitler's Army still fought the Four Powers—Britain, the United States, France and the Soviet Union—on all fronts. Three days after Austria pulled out of the Third Reich, Hitler committed suicide in a bunker underneath a Berlin that had practically ceased to exist. Germany surrendered on May 8, 1945.

When the smoke of Allied bombings cleared, Vienna fared better than Berlin. Eighty percent of the houses and apartments in Vienna were still standing in 1945, though a full 270,000 people were homeless. About 12,000 had died in the bombings. Those who had lived soon risked starvation, since both rail and road lines to farms in the countryside were blocked or destroyed. The population planted fields of vegetables in parks or tried to buy what they could in the black market that had sprung up in 1944. Refugees from Eastern Europe fled

Soviet control and flooded into Austria with hopes of protection under the wing of the Western powers. Jews who had survived Hitler's extermination efforts in the East also made their way back to Austria and Germany. They fled as well, from deadly pogroms by Poles and others that began almost as soon as the war was over. Some Jews hoped to be smuggled into British-controlled Palestine.

Only about 4,000 Jews remained in Austria in the months after the war ended, compared to the 160,000 Jews who had lived there before the war. Some outlived the war by hiding in attics and cellars. Others had married Christians, posed as Christians during the war, or were children of mixed marriages. Only about 1,700 Jews survived the concentration camps. The Nazi goal of a land "clean" of Jews had nearly succeeded in Austria.

In July, Austria and Vienna's city centers were divided into separate zones by the four victorious powers, though the country itself was never divided into east and west as Germany was later. In October, the Western Allies recognized the provisional government set up by the Soviets, and on November 25, Austria had its first national elections since 1930. Because ex-Nazi Party members were forbidden from voting or putting forth political candidates, electoral success came to the Socialist Party and to the conservative Austrian People's Party. The communists won 5 percent of the vote.

The new government was made up largely of former anti-Nazi Austrian conservatives and fascists, as well as socialists who had been jailed and persecuted in the 1930s. Despite their ideological differences, post-war politicians agreed on one issue that would weigh upon Austria up to the present: Austria was Hitler's first victim, coerced into the Anschluss. Under international law, according to "first victim" logic, post-war Austria was not responsible for what had happened on its soil between 1938 and 1945. This premise became a national obsession to rewrite the recent past, to cleanse Austria of national guilt for the Nazi atrocities in which the country took part.

It was the Western powers who had first crafted the myth of Austria as first victim in the Moscow Declaration of 1943. After the war, Austria was considered a liberated country. With an eye on future war reparations, the Soviets had insisted in the Moscow Declaration that Austria take responsibility for fighting willingly with Hitler: "Austria is reminded, however, that she has a responsibility which she cannot evade for participating in the war on the side of Hitlerite Germany, and that in the final settlement account will inevitably be taken of her own contribution to her liberation." The State Treaty in 1955 that restored Austria to its full independence, however stated that "No reparation shall be exacted from Austria arising out of the existence of a state of war in Europe after 1^s September 1939." It also ordered Austria to return all property and restore the legal rights of people persecuted on Austrian soil because of race or religion. Six months after the treaty was signed, all property of Jews and others persecuted under the Nazis which had not been claimed was turned over to the Austrian government, which forwarded it to organizations set up to provide relief to Nazi victims.

Under pressure from the Allies, many laws were enacted to codify the return of property and rights to those persecuted under the Nazis. Of greatest interest in the case of Guido's library and the Mahler manuscript was the Third Restitution Act of 1947, which covered forced sale of property and "Aryanizations." A legal summary of the Restitution Act stated that the law assumed all property taken from Nazi victims had been taken illegally: "Thus, the burden of proof is placed upon the present holder of property to show that the property had been acquired independently of the takeover of power by the Nazi Regime." This act, however, allowed claims for restitution only up until 1956. The restitution laws had their weak points, one of them being that property in the hands of someone who did not know it was stolen by the Nazis could retain it, even if the rightful owner or heir eventually appeared with proof of ownership.

After the war, as the American Jewish Committee put it, "It was not easy to claim reparations from a 'victim.'" Because of its first victim status, Austria admitted no legal responsibility to compensate victims of the Nazis. The country felt ambivalent about fulfilling the promises contained in the restitution laws. When it came to claiming property, Jewish victims and their heirs faced protracted negotiations, misinformation from the Austrian government and refusals to return what was theirs. This was especially true when art and other cultural objects were involved. Post-war Austria clung to its cultural heritage as an antidote against its Nazi past, and the country thought it in the public interest to hold onto its cultural treasures no matter how they had been acquired. Austrian museums and collectors had purchased thousands of looted art objects during the war, objects that post-war Austria often refused outright to return to owners and heirs. The Rothschild family was forced to "give" Austria certain paintings in exchange for the return and export of other objects the family had lost to the Nazis. Austria did the same trade with the family of Ferdinand Bloch-Bauer, a prominent Viennese collector who had to give the country paintings by Gustav Klimt in exchange for a visa to export other artwork.

A confidential U.S. State Department memo from 1950 found that thousands of paintings whose origins could have been suspect were stored out of sight in the basement of the Viennese public auction house, the Dorotheum, which was said to be the most important "fence" for looted art treasures during the war. Austria also hid a quarter of a million books looted from Jewish homes by the Nazis in the basement of the imperial palace in Vienna. In 1955, "Austrian officials quietly began distributing more than 186,000 of the looted books to their own governmental network of libraries—among them the official library of the Austrian chancellor." My father Achim struggled for years with the Austrian government to reclaim parts of the Adler library that had landed in the National Library of Vienna and other public institutions. Of the more than $1

billion worth of Jewish assets taken by the Austrians under the
Nazi regime, the Austrian government today admits that only
a small portion was returned to Jewish owners and heirs.

After the war, the Western powers concentrated more on
the rehabilitation of Germany than on its small southern
neighbor. Because the Soviets had already taken over much of
Eastern Europe and showed no inclination to offer those lands
independence, the Allies felt they needed a strong Germany
and Austria as soon as possible as a buffer zone between Soviet
might and Western democracies. Austria lost no time in
defining itself as the last bastion of democracy in central Europe,
and in its desire to ward off communism, the country worked
hard to erase its fascist National Socialist past. Under Allied
pressure, the Austrian government banned the Nazi Party and
affiliates, and members had to register. Several war tribunals
were set up. The Austrians made a distinction between Nazi
Party members who joined the party out of commitment to
Nazism, and those who were forced to join through coercion
or to maintain their jobs. All ex-Nazis who had joined the party
before 1938 were fired from certain professions and from all
civil service jobs. Higher Nazi Party officials received higher
penalties than the rank-and-file Nazis. In the end, these
denazification efforts proved so unpopular with Austrians that
most Nazis were amnestied in 1948.

Despite denazification efforts and laws designed to
recompense Jews for persecution, post-war Austrians still
manifested an unhealthy dose of the antisemitism that had
plagued them during the war. In U.S. surveys in 1947 and 1948
about 40 percent of people surveyed in Vienna, Salzburg and
Linz claimed that the "Jewish character was responsible for
antisemitism." About a third of the people surveyed in Vienna
and nearly half in Linz believed the Jews in displaced person
camps were "profiteers," benefiting too much from Allied help
at the expense of Austrians. Jewish displaced persons in Austria
never accounted for more than 10 percent of the whole, yet
Austrians held them responsible for the hunger and housing

shortages in the country. In still another survey, half of the Austrians polled claimed the Nazis had gone too far persecuting the Jews, but that "something had to be done to place limits on them." Surveys in Germany yielded similar results.

As an anti-Nazi Austrian in Germany, Rudolf von Ficker, one of my Aunt Melanie's last friends, knew that wartime antisemitism in the former Reich would not simply disappear now that the war had been lost. Yet as a professor, he had some hope in the young Germans who worked hard at their studies in an academic environment free of National Socialism. Ficker taught at the University of Munich in a musicology department that barely existed in the bombed-out city. "There is no institute anymore, not a single book," Ficker wrote to the Oxford exile Egon Wellesz, Jewish Austrian musicologist, composer and former student of my grandfather. "There are no resources at all for the entire academic faculty," he continued. "And the teaching takes place in lecture halls that can't be heated either and that are improvised and patched together out of rubble. There's not a single library left that one could work at. However, the students display an immense will to work, a will that is rather touching in its pointlessness."

Three years after my aunt's deportation, Ficker could not forget how Erich Schenk was implicated in her presumed death. He wrote that his Munich students had an "honest desire to return to a clean way of living—a Schenk would be unthinkable here!"

On October 29, 1945, Ficker sent a memo to the state government in the northern Austrian region of Tirol regarding Melanie's death and Schenk's "acquisition" of my grandfather's library for the University of Vienna. The memo laid out the story as I've told it here, though Ficker added at the end his reason for bringing the topic up to the authorities:

In hindsight on the friendly relations that bound me to my teacher Prof. Dr. Guido Adler and his relations, as well as in the interest of the

reputation of Austrian science, I consider it my duty to make known the
aforementioned state of affairs. I am convinced that aside from me, all
foreign representatives of the subject out of basic decency will sharply
disapprove of the brutal actions of Herr Prof. Schenk, and will condemn
all contact with this representative of Austrian musicology.

In other words, Ficker implied that Schenk could cause bad international press for the new, supposedly anti-Nazi Austria. Furthermore, he was prepared to show Melanie's letters as proof of his accusations against Schenk. At first, the authorities did little with Ficker's information.

The University of Vienna also seemed to care little about Schenk's Nazi connections and the confiscation of the Adler library. Some committed lower-level Nazi Party members were fired from the faculty, including Alfred Orel who had first led the Gestapo to my grandfather's house. But most of the professors and administration who had worked under the Nazis remained after the war. It must be kept in mind that in Austria, universities were always a part of the national civil service, professorial appointments being confirmed by the government. Therefore, the pre-Nazi Austrian government, and later the Nazis, had the power to hire or fire university professors. After Germany entered Austria in 1938, "the best Austrian scholars were banned from the universities, though removals, especially in the social sciences, had occurred in the preceding years as well," as a study of post-war Austrian universities points out. The holes in Nazi-era Austrian faculties were filled by moving loyal lower-ranking scholars up, or by importing ideologically "sound" professors from Germany.

This was true especially in Vienna. Schenk received his prestigious appointment to my grandfather's Musicology Seminar in this way. Under the Nazis, all professors had to join the Party or one of its organs in order to retain their jobs. After the war, universities would have been nearly empty of faculty if everyone involved with the Nazis had been fired. So instead of banning all ex-Nazis, the government ordered the dismissal of all Germans who had been appointed to the universities after the 1938 Anschluss. Schenk was Austrian, not German, and despite the fact that he had worked at the university in Rostock before his appointment to the University of Vienna in 1940, he fell between the cracks of the post-war denazification laws.

It became Rudolf von Ficker's personal mission to discover why Schenk was allowed to remain in Vienna when there was so much evidence of his complicity with Nazis and the Gestapo. Schenk had confiscated his own personnel file from the university, so it may be impossible ever to know exactly how he kept his position. But perhaps his post-war connections were as influential as his wartime ones had been. As a study on post-war universities notes: "The main techniques used to retain university positions were: (1) affidavits (Persilscheine) from former victims of the Nazi oppression, which were the most effective, and (2) support from local politicians, priests or even better, from bishops or members of high society. Through these, even some German citizens kept their positions. Social capital . . . became more relevant than guilt or academic reputation."

By 1946, Ficker moved to his former home Igls near Innsbruck. Munich having become too depressing for him, he hoped to regain his position at the University of Innsbruck. "My closest colleague, Kurt Huber, the psychophysicist and folklorist was executed there [Munich]," he wrote to Wellesz in April. Huber had been the mentor of the White Rose resistance group, run by a group of students including Hans Scholl, his sister Sophie and Christoph Probst, who were also executed. Ficker continued: "On top of that, there were the bomb raids that destroyed everything built up over twelve years." From Igls, Ficker launched his campaign to get Schenk removed from his post for his dealings with my Aunt Melanie, and the story is revealed in a series of letters he wrote to Wellesz between 1946 and 1948.

In an effort to get the government to take a close look at Schenk, Ficker went to the Ministry of Education, which oversaw university appointments. In February 1946, he wrote about the case to Otto Baron von Skrbenksy. Skrbensky had been a pre-war fascist and had become a strong supporter of the newfound Austrian nationalism that encouraged Austrians to do everything they could—from abandoning standard "high German" (Hochdeutsch) to wearing traditional costumes—to distinguish themselves from Germans. It was largely men like Skrbensky who carried on the tradition of fascism in post-war Austria, as a recent study notes: "In the academic sphere even more than in other areas, there was the almost uninterrupted continuity of the Catholic Austrian variety of fascism . . . and this continuity was embodied in the person of Otto (Baron von) Skrbensky, the Austrio-fascist university functionary who was a powerful section chief in the years after 1945." Ficker had some idea of what sort of man he was dealing with; in his memo explaining my Aunt Melanie's case, Ficker parried an argument Skrbensky might make in favor of Schenk:

Prof. Schenk and his representatives always claimed they "saved" the library for the "Ostmark"[Nazi term for Austria]. Under normal circumstances such a reason might be plausible and laudable. But in this case it is obvious that the need to save her life was the sole reason why Ms. Adler had no choice but to offer up the library where she had the chance. Under the barbaric circumstances of the time, anyone whose feelings were ruled by justice rather than Nazism would have acted humanely, not according to his own gain.

Ficker's outrage against Schenk had not cooled:

In contrast, Prof. Schenk has embraced the most despicable and contemptible strategies the Nazis had bred: The unscrupulous pillaging, ostracising and destruction of people with different attitudes or merely different racial background. He covered up his blackmailing behavior with the pretext of some—not even applicable—need for local prestige without wasting a thought on the human life at stake. It doesn't really matter if these actions happened in the alleged interest of a public institution. What does matter is that Prof. Schenk had no scruples whatsoever when he used his power of authority as head of the institute to serve Nazism's brutal methods of Aryanization. And against the very man who had founded the institute and who had established its reputation worldwide.

By April 21, 1946, the authorities seem to have begun proceedings against Schenk. Yet in June, Schenk was nominated for full membership to the prestigious Austrian Academy of Sciences "for his merits in the acquisition of the Adler library." Ficker wrote to the *Internationale Gesellschaft für Musikwissenschaften* (International Society for Musicology) explaining Schenk's complicity, and urging them to protest Schenk's nomination. Instead, the Academy appointed Schenk to head up its music research and publications departments.

Ficker's cries for justice in my aunt's case quickly made him unpopular at the Ministry of Education. Austria, after all, wanted to deny it had anything to do with Nazis, the Gestapo, confiscations and concentration camps. Yet Skrbensky met with Ficker in June or July 1946 to discuss the Adler affair. Ficker later reported Skrbensky's view of the case: "Schenk had stated that all the detailed accusations Mely made in her letters to me were nothing but lies." Proof was the letter of gratitude my aunt had written to Schenk in 1941 when she believed he had helped her father fight eviction in the month before his death. "The authorities have taken this letter as valid proof that Mely's accusations were without legal foundation," Ficker wrote. After their meeting, Ficker sent a follow-up letter to Skrbensky that explained Schenk's "infamous white-washing attempt."

When Ms. Adler refused her consent [to sell the library to Schenk], however, there was no further need for Prof. Schenk to shrink from this alternative, more brutal way. After all, he held proof that provided him with a moral alibi for the future once the heir to the library was done away with: Ms. Adler's letter of gratitude . . .

Professor Schenk has indeed used this piece of evidence successfully . . . He had many chances in the past to prove the noble spirit with which the murder victim had certified him. He could have joined the circle of people who made it their purpose to save Ms. Adler from her imminent doom.

I have always identified Prof. Schenk as being the one who destroyed these efforts.

Chapter Eleven

VOICES IN THE DARK

Egon Wellesz sensed even more than Rudolf von Ficker how important Melanie's letters were in the case against Erich Schenk. My aunt's own voice arose out of these letters—her fears, her suspicions, her conviction that Schenk and Heiserer had collaborated against her. Aside from the letters, Ficker had no documented evidence of the betrayal that had sent Melanie to the deportation trains.

In 1946, Wellesz advised Ficker to make copies of Melanie's letters and send them to Oxford where Wellesz lived and taught. As a former student of Guido's and an Austrian musicologist himself, he supported Ficker's quest to reveal the true story of Melanie's death and the Adler library's confiscation. The reputation of Austrian musicology was at stake if the international community discovered that Schenk, one of Austria's top musicologists, had committed crimes during the war. Wellesz wanted to read the evidence for himself, but no doubt he considered copying Melanie's letters a prudent security measure. If Melanie's letters were lost, the investigation into Schenk would be, too.

Ficker didn't act fast enough. On September 27, a French official arrived at his home in Igls-Innsbruck and confiscated all of my Aunt Melanie's letters. As an Austrian subject to the Allied occupation forces, Ficker could not refuse to hand them over. "Naturally I was very worried about this until I got news from Vienna that the documents had come into the hands of the authorities in charge of the investigation," he wrote to Wellesz in October.

In September, Schenk and his friends at the University of Vienna went on the defensive. Wellesz must have made enough noise from England to catch Schenk's attention; he received a letter from Schenk's attorney that contained "a threat to intimidate you [Wellesz]," as Ficker mentioned in a return note to Wellesz. What the threat entailed is not known. More powerful still was the whisper campaign against Ficker that accused him of pursuing Schenk not to right the wrongs of the war, but to advance his own career. After the war the Allies requested that universities invite Jewish and other anti-Nazi professors who had been fired by the Nazis to return to their pre-war posts. Austria seldom informed the scholars of this right, especially if they had emigrated.

In 1946, Ficker wished to return to the University of Innsbruck, where he had founded the musicology institute in the 1920s. The last man to hold the post was Wilhelm Fischer, a Jew who was fired by the Nazi authorities in 1938. Fischer lived through the war and knew of his right to return to Innsbruck, but he didn't wish to. The Ministry of Education considered offering him a post as head of the University of Vienna's Musicology Seminar—Schenk's position—so that Innsbruck would be free to take on Ficker. A ministry memo of January 4, 1945 that voiced this plan also noted that Schenk was "not politically flawless," implying his Nazi connections and sympathies. Yet the plan came to nothing and Fischer eventually found a more lucrative post-war position at the Conservatorium in Vienna. Despite the fact that the Innsbruck position was still empty and Ficker was ready to fill it, the Austrian bureaucracy needed confirmation that Fischer no longer wanted it.

By October, Fischer had not shown up in Innsbruck for the third straight semester, and Ficker had been nominated unanimously by the university staff to fill the empty post. But the Ministry of Education took so long to confirm his new post that Ficker suspected Schenk had some influence either with the ministry or with Skrbensky. Though living in Austria, Ficker was still officially connected to the University of Munich. He had not taught or been paid in a year. In November, he finally returned to Munich to teach "under the most depressing circumstances" in order to earn some money. He clearly believed that his exile in Munich was part of Schenk's defensive action against him. "I was to be deported," Ficker wrote Wellesz, "and therefore my appointment to the post here [in Innsbruck] had to be prevented."

Ficker and Wellesz were not the only scholars with an eye on the Adler-Schenk case. Friedrich Hayek, a Viennese living in London who would later win the Nobel Prize in economics, believed Schenk really was being investigated by conscientious Austrian authorities. He wrote to Fritz Saxl, a Viennese art historian at London's Warburg Institute, on October 17, 1946: "The accusations against Professor Schenk are well known and have been carefully investigated by the responsible officials in the Ministry of Education who have expressly asked me to supply any further evidence which I can get hold of; but up to the present the results of the investigations have been entirely negative." The main reason for this, Hayek wrote, was that the authorities continued to consider Melanie's letter of gratitude as proof of Schenk's good intentions. Wellesz wrote to Saxl that Ficker had enough evidence to prove that Melanie's letter of gratitude "is annulled by the letters which she wrote later."

Hayek's conversations with the Ministry of Education made him waiver in his conviction that Ficker could actually prove

his case against Schenk: "Vague accusations of all kinds are
made against almost everybody, and when it comes to a question
of definite evidence, none is usually forthcoming. I am
personally satisfied that the will to punish people guilty of crimes
is present, and that all that is needed is adequate proof of
what they have done." Hayek also wrote to Wellesz, who
forwarded one of his notes to Ficker. On October 30, Ficker
wrote Wellesz that "Hayek gets his information from Skrbensky
who still quotes Mely's letter as decisive counter-evidence against
his accusations—despite my extensive explanation of the case!
If the dealings in this case were left in his [Skrbensky's] hands
nothing would ever be resolved."

Ficker was heartened, nevertheless, by some good news:
the English and the Americans were investigating the Schenk-
Adler case independent of Skrbenky's ministry. Even my father
Achim, who had hired an attorney to sell the Adler houses in
Vienna and find the remnants of my grandfather's library, had
ordered his attorney to look into Schenk and the Musicology
Seminar. On December 4, 1946, Hayek received a letter from
Skrbensky that laid out the status of the case against Schenk.
Hayek replied with his own comments in English in the margins
of the letter. Skrbensky had begun by declaring that the
investigation thus far had turned up nothing against Schenk
in the matter of the Adler library. "The persons nominated to
give information relevant to the presentation of evidence
against Professor Schenk have partly acquitted him of the
charges brought against him and have clearly testified in his
favor," to which Hayek responded, *Prof. Ficker was not allowed to
take part in the process.* Skrbenksy continued: "The other witnesses
who tried to give incriminating testimony simply gave
suppositions, and they were not able to rely on their own
perceptions or to cite evidence for their claims." Hayek:
Nonsense! Skrbensky: "In addition, the group of witnesses who
put forward incriminating testimony consisted exclusively of
persons who had arguments or sharp differences with Professor
Schenk for personal reasons." Hayek: *Does he mean Ficker?*

Skrbensky obviously had accepted Schenk's argument that Ficker persecuted him to advance his own career, not out of a sense of justice. Skrbensky added that he was surprised at some of the witnesses against Schenk, who had shady political records, "including an SS officer who is charged with war crimes." (It isn't known who this was.) Skrbensky stated again that Schenk's letter of gratitude from Melanie canceled the value of Ficker's incriminating letters from Melanie, and he even made clear that the University of Vienna's possession of the Adler library was not a mark against Schenk. "After all, it was in Austria's best interest that he save the library for our country. Incidentally, Professor Schenk has already taken measures to register the library in accordance with the existing regulations for the registration of property confiscated by the National Socialists." Hayek commented: *Of course, because Adler's son claims the library which was stolen by Schenk. But Munich wanted to buy the library and to guarantee Melly Adlers life[sic].*

Skrbensky next made a comment that must have incensed Ficker when he got word of it: "Many witnesses, all of them enemies of National Socialism by the way, have stated that Ms. Adler was not of sound mind towards the end and that several measures against her could have been avoided had this not been the case." Hayek: *Her letters show that she knew exactly what "transport were sent to Poland" [meant] and that this would be her fate.* Blaming the victim for her own treatment was a popular argument used by Austrians of the period against the Jews in general. Many thought the Jews had brought the Nazi persecutions on themselves. Skrbensky didn't elaborate on what "several measures" could have been spared against Melanie, but he came dangerously close to blaming her for her own deportation and execution.

On January 28, 1947 my Aunt Melanie was declared officially dead by the Austrian court in Vienna. This was the result of a petition my father filed through an attorney in Vienna while we were living in New Jersey. Until then she had been considered a missing person, like so many others who had been killed in the Nazi executions. More than a year and a half had passed since the end of the war and the liberation of the concentration camps, enough time for my Aunt Melanie to surface in Vienna or elsewhere if she was still alive. The District Court of Vienna declared that "Dr. Melanie Adler did not survive May 8, 1945"—the surrender of the Third Reich.

The official declaration that the heiress of the Adler library was dead did nothing to fuel the case against Schenk, however. As Ficker informed Wellesz in May 1947: "The Schenk affair seems to have been put to sleep completely." Ficker assumed enough time had passed for the authorities to have copied the letters that had been confiscated the previous September; he now wanted them back. The authorities in Vienna gave him no response. "I have the impression that the sudden confiscation of the letters was nothing but a manoeuvre to do away with the affair by deleting the incriminating documents," Ficker wrote on May 6.

Ficker had admitted in previous letters that he was tired of the Schenk situation, and wished he had never demanded an investigation. His disaffection could be traced in part to the strain the controversy had put on his professional life and on his perceptions in general; at times, Ficker seemed to see conspiracies in the most unlikely places. That heightened sense of suspicion was clear in a comment about my father to Wellesz:

About Achim A: I haven't heard from him since autumn. But recently I was told that he cancelled the mandate of his attorney, Dr. Walter Redlich of Vienna. I couldn't rule out the possibility that Sch[enk] might have tried to come to an arrangement with him directly, and I've recently asked Achim for an explanation. He didn't really seem all that moved by his sister's death, and that's why I think it might be possible that he is only interested in settling the affair for his material gain, not for the sake of his sister.

There is no evidence that my father or his attorney ever

negotiated with Schenk, but it is true that my father tried to find out the whereabouts and condition of all Adler family property in Vienna. As his representative in Vienna, the attorney Hans Wiala replaced Redlich, and continued to look into the existing assets of the Adlers. The Lannerstrasse house had been occupied during the war but was empty in 1945. My father's former home and medical practice on Gonzagagasse had been damaged during bombing raids. Because of the unstable real estate situation in Vienna after the war, he was obliged to sell his portion of the houses at a fraction of their value.

Some of my grandfather's possessions sat in boxes at a depot on Singerstrasse in Vienna. The depot had been partly plundered by the Soviets when they first occupied the city, and in June 1945, a Regional Tax Authority Office official noted that broken boxes, dishes, pictures and frames were among other confiscated items that had not belonged to Guido. "But it is striking that especially the books, precisely the incomplete editions of classic books, prayer books in Hebrew, books written in English and also a music history by Dr. Guido Adler, were nearly all stolen," the official wrote. He also noted that Reich officials had "ordered the transfer without remuneration of the large library, the manuscript collection, the collection of original letters by Bruckner, Mahler and other renowned musicians, to the Musicology Department of the University of Vienna."

In July 1947, Schenk prepared an inventory for the Tax Office that listed everything the Musicology Seminar still had of my grandfather's library. The list was small and included two inlaid book cases, four bookshelves, an easy chair, two framed pictures and a collection of plaques. The large number of books that the seminar actually possessed was mentioned only later; Schenk's excuse was a lack of staff to do a book-by-book inventory. One sensational item Schenk listed was a death mask of Beethoven, authenticated by the seal of the Beethovenhaus in Bonn. Although the university returned the items on Schenk's list to Wiala's care in 1948, the Beethoven death mask was not among them. Only two masks are known to still be in existence today: one in the Beethovenhaus, another at the City Museum of Vienna. The Viennese museum had acquired its death mask in 1887 from Franz Liszt's estate. The Beethovenhaus has not provided information about the provenance of its own mask and the possibility of other authenticated copies.

Schenk's inventory of items belonging to my grandfather was far shorter than the one attorney Wiala presented to the Tax Office. Wiala's included 13 oil paintings, many portraits and family photographs, 10 boxes containing porcelain and glass, 3 boxes with dishes and vases, a box of musicology books, a damaged box of music manuscripts that included Beethoven scores, and a travel basket with family mementos such as photos and diplomas. Missing from Wiala's list was a specific reference to the Mahler manuscript.

The University of Vienna had apparently shared the loot of my grandfather's property with other Viennese institutions. After the war, the National Library of Vienna had 51 bundles of documents that Schenk characterized as "private correspondence, correspondence in regard to the Handbook for Music History, composition manuscripts, etc." The libraries of both the Society of Music Friends and the Academy for Music and the Performing Arts in Vienna were also said to have some parts of his library. Ficker had warned Melanie that Guido's library would be scattered if it fell into Schenk's hands. It happened just as he had predicted. The portion of the library stored at the Austrian National Library was under the control of Leopold Nowak, an avowed Nazi and Schenk supporter who resisted my father's efforts to retrieve it. After five years of wrangling, my father succeeded in importing a portion of it to the United States in 1951 and selling it to the University of Georgia, which used it to found a musicology library. The collection came to about 1,200 titles published between about 1875 and 1930. In 1952, the University of Georgia also acquired a portion of my grandfather's collection of personal letters. Edward Reilly, who catalogued the correspondence and wrote of my grandfather and Gustav Mahler's friendship, wrote later that the entire collection filled 74 boxes. The letters to or from Alexius Meinong, Siegfried Wagner, Richard Strauss as well as Gustav and Alma Mahler are evidence of Guido's wide friendships and correspondence with prominent people of his day.

On August 2, 1954, Rudolf von Ficker died in Igls-Innsbruck at the age of 68. He never saw justice done to the men he believed had murdered my Aunt Melanie and stolen my grandfather's library. In an undated letter from just after the war, Egon Wellesz had written that Ficker was "universally respected, both as a scholar and as a man of integrity." Richard Heiserer senior died on August 17, 1957. He had received no punishment for his membership in the Nazi Party or his relationship with the Gestapo. In his post-war denazification proceedings, a Jewish woman reportedly had written a letter in his favor saying Heiserer had been anti-Nazi and had helped Jews. Heiserer himself had claimed he was a victim of the Nazi regime when the Gestapo forbade him to leave Vienna for five months in 1942 because they believed he had helped an unnamed Jewish girl. He subsequently admitted that he had been the one to inform the Gestapo that the girl was Jewish in the first place.

At the commission, Heiserer complained about the Nazi rule to report which of his prospective clients were Jewish; it cost him money when he wasn't allowed to represent Jewish clients. The Austrian government hesitated to punish ex-Nazi Party members who had been required to join because of their profession, and who had joined after 1938. Heiserer fell into both categories. He escaped censure for his acts during the war, and died leaving the Mahler manuscript as an inheritance to his then 14-year-old son, Richard Heiserer junior.

Erich Schenk went on to a glittering career in Vienna's academia. In 1957, he became the first musicologist to act as rector of the University of Vienna. Until 1971, he continued to head the Musicology Seminar that Guido Adler had helped found. He died on October 11, 1974, his unscrupulous acts during World War II unpunished.

Chapter Twelve

THE RECKONING

Nearly a century had passed between Gustav Mahler's birthday gift to my grandfather, and my own journey to Vienna to see the once lost manuscript of "*Ich bin der Welt abhanden gekommen*" with my own eyes. As I flew over the Atlantic in October of 2000, I looked down at the ocean that I had first crossed by ship as an infant fleeing Vienna with my family more than sixty years before. Over the years, I had visited Vienna as a tourist, and it was always a whimsical homecoming. I spent most of my time wandering the streets and thinking about what my life would have been like if there had been no war. I would have moved in fairly privileged circles—a perk of being the grandson of the famous Guido Adler and the son of a physician. I imagined myself sitting in coffee houses discussing important issues of the day with intelligent, beautiful people. My parents would have entertained friends in our comfortable home, perhaps even at the Lannerstrasse villa, which my father might have inherited. I would come home in the afternoon to the sounds of my mother playing Chopin in the parlor. As I grew older, maybe I would have spent evenings with friends in a tavern in the Grinzing area, drinking wine and listening to awful accordion music. Perhaps my grandfather Guido would have lived longer if there had been no Anschluss; maybe I would have known him a little, enough to have my own memories of him. Certainly I would have known my Aunt Melanie, who kept my picture on her mirror until she was deported.

But the Anschluss did happen, and my childhood in the United States differed radically from the Viennese fantasies that I spun later in life. After arriving almost penniless in New York, we had lived in a series of dingy, basement apartments. My father moved from state to state, often leaving us behind while he completed the studies and internships he needed to receive his American medical license. My mother worked as a photographer's assistant and at night she sewed military braid for officer's uniforms. Some weeks, we ate little more than rice and peas. By the time I had graduated from high school in Arizona, we had lived in twenty-eight apartments and several houses in six different states. It was only natural that I dreamed of an idealized Vienna where my family had roots, social status and security.

The feelings of nostalgia—of what could have been—came to a halt during a visit to Vienna in the mid-1980s. I had visited the Mauthausen concentration camp near Vienna, which had been turned into a museum. The camp sat beside the small town of the same name, and had been the killing ground for 200,000 people by the end of the war. Photos showed the large gas containers the Nazis needed to feed the chambers. The gas arrived by trains that passed right beside the town. What of the townspeople in Mauthausen and other towns along the railroad tracks? How could they possibly not have known what was happening? How could 200,000 human beings be killed in a small village setting in the beautiful Austrian countryside without it being common knowledge? Could the Austrians have been so blind? I realized then . . . of course they knew. My wistful thoughts of life as an Austrian ended that day.

My wife Louise, youngest son David and I arrived in Vienna on Tuesday, October 10. After settling in at the hotel, I decided to stretch my legs. Outside, I noticed the sign on the cross street: Wipplingerstrasse. My Aunt Melanie had given that street as her address when she hid from the Gestapo in the last weeks of her life. I quickly crossed the street and walked up to the first old building near the corner. The number on the side of the building, 24, stopped me in my tracks. This was Wipplingerstrasse 24, the exact building that my Aunt Melanie had claimed as her last address before her deportation. Through some strange coincidence, I had booked a hotel 100 feet away from what was possibly my aunt's last home. Wipplingerstrasse 24 had been turned into an office building, and I went in and wandered the halls, trying to get a sense of what it must have been like for Melanie. Even with the whir of business machines, neon lights and workers occupied with their various tasks, I somehow sensed my aunt's presence—and felt her fear.

We spent the rest of the week meeting with a variety of people. I had researched Viennese lawyers before leaving the United States, and after an hour's meeting with attorney Alfred Noll, I retained him as my representative in the Mahler manuscript dispute. Noll was bright, tough and had a good sense of humor. He had also represented several other people in their attempts to recover property stolen during the war; he had no qualms about taking on a cause that was not popular in Vienna. My Aunt Lisl had also met us in Vienna, and on the following evening, we all had dinner with the historian Brigitte Hamann.

Things were starting to happen. *Profil* magazine in Vienna had found out about the Mahler controversy before I even arrived in Vienna. An article complete with photos came out while I was there, and I was pleased to see it was favorable to my case. It also threw the light of day onto the issue, rather than allowing the people involved to operate away from the public eye. Ruth Pleyer from the Holocaust Victims Information and Support Center gave me the results of research she had done in the archives in Vienna. She had found out details about Richard Heiserer senior's involvement with the Nazi Party. Now I knew there was more to Heiserer junior's story than he had told me.

We also met with Ernst Bacher, head of the Monument Office, who had declared the Mahler manuscript to be a national treasure, thus prohibiting it from leaving the country. In his large, ornate office, Bacher politely explained how the decision had been made. I then asked a question: Since the Mahler manuscript had been in the private possession first of Gustav Mahler, then my grandfather, and had never been in the public domain, how could the Austrian government decide it could never leave Austria? It is important to preserve Austrian culture, Bacher replied. So much for individual property rights.

This was just a taste of the Austrian system of justice. Over time, I had others. To file a lawsuit, the plaintiff has to post with the court an amount of money based on the percentage of the value of the case. This has prevented many Holocaust survivors from even attempting to recover their family's possessions; they simply can't afford the cost of filing suit. Instead of being presented to a jury, civil cases are decided only by judges who are part of the civil service system. But perhaps worst of all, there is no pre-trial discovery. Attorneys can't request depositions or documents, or use other means of finding out the truth of a case from the opposition. Ever since Heiserer junior had claimed that his father received the Mahler manuscript as a fee, I had been looking forward to asking him questions and getting documents from him relevant to the case. It was not to be. In American courts, lawyers call that trial by ambush. I kept thinking about all of the art that was missing from my grandfather's house. Where was it? I couldn't ask the man who might know.

Toward the end of the week, we dropped by Sotheby's auction house, where I asked to see the Mahler manuscript. They refused. But our appearance must have caused some hurried discussions between Sotheby's management and its lawyers, for I later found a message at my hotel informing me Sotheby's would arrange a meeting between me and Heiserer junior, the man who claimed ownership of the manuscript.

The meeting took place on the following Monday, October 16. I arrived with Alfred Noll and my son David at the offices of Sotheby's legal counsel, where we were met by the Sotheby's attorney Richard Kustor and his young associate. Another representative of Sotheby's waited for us in a small, unpretentious conference room. After a few minutes, Richard Heiserer arrived. He was a short man, middle aged, with a rather worn, world-weary face. I wondered if he looked like his father. If so, I was seeing a face similar to the one Melanie had seen many times when she fought for her inheritance. I had been told that Heiserer specialized in traffic accident cases. He appeared ill at ease with an international dispute over the ownership of an exceptional music manuscript. With him was his wife, a younger woman who was surprisingly well dressed and attractive compared to her husband. Both avoided looking at me. When Kustor introduced us, I offered my hand to Heiserer. He refused it, only acknowledging my greeting with a nod. I sensed it was more than bad manners—nothing reveals nervousness like a damp, clammy handshake. Heiserer and his wife settled at the conference table as far from the rest of us as possible. He never once looked me in the eye.

We could not speak to each other directly. I knew very little German, and Heiserer, though he had claimed knowledge of English on his resumé, chose not to demonstrate it at the meeting. Kustor, Sotheby's attorney, tried to lessen the tension in the room. I had to ask Noll several times what was being said. Everyone in the room knew that the Mahler case would not be resolved at the conference table, but that didn't stop me from dropping a bomb into Heiserer's lap. My attorney informed him that if he agreed, we would be prepared to donate the Mahler manuscript to an Austrian public institution.

Heiserer quietly looked down and grinned. I could guess what he was thinking: *Who is this guy kidding?* He shook his head, then confirmed with his voice: No deal. Noll then pointed out that the academic community was interested in seeing a copy of the manuscript. Would Heiserer allow a copy of it to be made? The same disbelieving smile crept over Heiserer's face: No deal. Philanthropy was obviously the farthest thing from his mind. To him, the Mahler wasn't about history, it was about money.

The meeting ended within 30 minutes. Nothing had been accomplished. That was no surprise considering Heiserer's conviction that his father had done nothing wrong during the war. My next move was to prove him wrong in court. As an American attorney, it was difficult for me to accept my powerlessness in the face of the roadblocks built into the Austrian judicial system. My frustration grew when I realized that 60 years after World War II, Austria has only just begun to reassess the role that it played in the Third Reich and its aftermath.

In 1998, Austria created a Historians Commission (*Historikerkommission*) to investigate whether the country had fulfilled its moral obligation to return assets and rights to Jews persecuted on Austrian soil during the war. It was a massive step for Austria to admit that the post-war Second Republic may not have acted as it should have. Ficker, my father Achim and many others had had to deal with a post-war Austria more concerned about its own victim status than the people it helped persecute. These issues are at present being scrutinized by the Commission, which has already released a portion of its findings.

The results have not been favorable to Austria. According to the reports, it intentionally made it difficult for Holocaust victims and their heirs to recover their property, findings that would have been no surprise to my father had he lived to see them. Furthermore, many Austrian Jews had lost not only property under the Nazis, but their citizenship as well. To avoid the vulnerable position of "stateless" people, most who emigrated became citizens of their adopted countries. After the war, Austria refused in many cases to restore Austrian citizenship to Jews who had been forced to give it up during the war. "This sent a clear signal that they were not wanted," the *Historikerkommission* said of those Jews who wanted to return to their homeland after the war. Only in the 1990s did Austria remedy the situation.

The Commission also found it unsettling that Austria was easily able to compute the wealth that had been in the hands of Jews in 1938, but could not say exactly how much of it had been returned to its rightful owners after the war. Without such statistics, it is only through conjecture that one can gauge how effective the restitution has been. Based on their research, historians estimate that only a small percentage of those pre-war assets have ever been restored to owners and heirs.

But things are changing. Austria has stepped up its efforts in the past decade or so, partly under pressure of class action lawsuits filed in the United States by Holocaust survivors or heirs. It may also be forced to demonstrate greater effort to help victims of the Third Reich because of the political fallout from both former Austrian President Kurt Waldheim and the right-wing reactionary Jorg Haider. There may also be a sense in Austria that the time to gain some absolution for its wartime acts is running out as the number of Holocaust victims dwindles. In 1998, the government announced that "Comprehensive compensation for the victims of Nazi injustice is in the interest of Austria."

In 1990, the Austrian Government Relief Fund provided up to $23 million to help elderly and frail Austrian Jews who had suffered during the Holocaust but live outside of Austria. In 2000, the Austrian Bank Fund was created to give up to $40 million in compensation to victims of the Nazis who lost bank accounts, private property and other assets during the war. Austria has also donated to Holocaust victims its remaining share of gold looted by the Nazis. In 2000 as well, Austria closed a highly publicized deal to aid surviving forced and slave laborers, whereby the Austrian Reconciliation Fund gives out funds collected from the Austrian government and companies

that benefited during the war from cheap or free labor. The
donations are considered voluntary, since Austria still holds to
the opinion that the country and its industry is only morally,
not legally, responsible for war crimes. Then in 2001, Austria
approved legislation that would "secure a final global resolution
of all remaining claims against Austria and/or Austrian
companies arising out of or related to the National Socialist
era or World War II." This General Settlement Fund offered
up to $480 million for restitution and social welfare cases of
Holocaust survivors and heirs. The fund does not address the
return of artworks stolen during the war.

For decades, Austria had been criticized for not doing
enough to return artwork looted by the Nazis. The first and
second "laws concerning works of art and cultural treasures"
(*Kunst-und Kulturgüterbereinigungsgesetz* of 1969 and 198
respectively) had been designed to restore art and cultural
treasures to Nazi victims and their heirs. But in the 1990s, about
8,000 looted artworks and artifacts were found still in Austria
possession in a monastery in the town of Mauerbach. Austria
claimed it had tried over the decades to locate the owners of
heirs of the art. In October 1996, what was unclaimed was
auctioned, earning about $13.5 million which was donated to
Jewish organizations in Austria.

In 1998, Austria passed a law that legislated the return of
artwork stolen by the Nazis and "which entered museums and
art collections under questionable circumstances." Austria had
been shaken from its complacency early in the year after
Manhattan district attorney impounded two Egon Schiele
paintings owned by Austria and on loan to the Museum of
Modern Art in New York. A Jewish family had stepped forward
and claimed the canvases were Nazi loot. The case sparked
debate about Austria's continued hoarding of stolen art, and
now it is combing through the artwork in state museums and
collections to see whether any were acquired secretly from the
Nazis. Some, including Degas' *Harlequin and Columbine* at the

Austrian Belvedere Gallery, are suspected of having been "Aryanized," in other words, sold far below market value, during the war. An index has been made of thousands of suspect pieces, including more than 900 at the Kunsthistorisches Museum in Vienna. Some have already been returned to owners or heirs as a result of the investigations. If Austria identifies looted artwork in its institutions but can't find the heirs, it must sell the works and donate the money to Jewish aid organizations.

Jewish families still have a difficult time proving ownership of stolen artwork, and tend to resort to lawsuits to retrieve their property. Only after decades of fighting, for example, has Austria agreed to return some 250 artworks and objects to the Viennese branch of the Rothschild family. A recent high-profile lawsuit was filed in California against the state of Austria to recover Gustav Klimt paintings once owned by the Jewish collector Ferdinand Bloch-Bauer, and which are now in possession of the Austrian Gallery. Austria protested that it has sovereign immunity from prosecution and could not be sued for events that happened before 1952. The California lower court decided that the lawsuit should proceed despite Austria's protests because, as the Art Newspaper characterized it, "the Klimts were taken in violation of international law—not just by Nazi 'Aryanization', but a second time when Austria itself required that the family donate paintings to it after the war in exchange for a license to export Ferdinand's remaining artworks." Bloch-Bauer's heir had first brought suit in Austria, but was forced to abandon the litigation when she was required to post her life savings with the court in order to proceed.

My own legal battle over the Mahler manuscript had barely begun when I found that the Mahler was not the only cultural artifact Heiserer had wanted to sell at Sotheby's. He had also presented them with the original manuscript of a story called "*Ich*" by the prominent Austrian Jewish author Arthur Schnitzler. I discovered this through Austrian court documents in December 2000, nearly two months after I had met with

Heiserer and Sotheby's officials in Vienna. I knew that my grandfather Guido had known Schnitzler, and this fact, combined with the "coincidence" that Heiserer had showed up with the Mahler and Schnitzler manuscripts at the same time, made me suspect that the Schnitzler might have also belonged to Guido. Why hadn't the auction house informed me of the Schnitzler manuscript before, and why had no one questioned its provenance when it was discovered that Heiserer might illegally possess the Mahler manuscript? Had Heiserer sold any artwork through Sotheby's in the past? Jonathan Olsoff, Sotheby's attorney in New York, sent me a reply to my questions on December 6:

Let me begin by assuring you that, upon learning of the questionable provenance of the Mahler Manuscript, Sotheby's immediately decided that it would not offer the Schnitzler manuscript for sale unless its provenance was clearly and unequivocally established. As it obviously occurred to us that the Schnitzler Manuscript may have also been part of the estate of Guido Adler, we carefully reviewed the information you had forwarded to us, which included an inventory of the property in Guido Adler's collection, to see if there was any reference to the Schnitzler Manuscript. There was no such reference. We also carefully examined the manuscript itself to see if it had any marking indicating that it had been part of Guido Adler's collection and did not find any such markings.

I thought how lucky it was that Mahler had written his birthday wishes to my grandfather on the manuscript of "*Ich bin der Welt abhanden gekommen.*" And how lucky it was that Guido had written about that musical gift, a clue that was discovered among his papers only many decades later. I had also been lucky to learn about the manuscript 95 years after it had been given to him. I hadn't been as lucky with the Schnitzler. Indeed, that manuscript may well have belonged to someone else who had fled the Nazis or had been exterminated. The Schnitzler issue brought home again the reality that private collections, art shops and museums all over the world hold art objects which, simply stated, don't belong there.

The resolution of the Mahler case must await a future edition of this story. The wheels of justice in Austria, as in America, grind slowly. The case is still pending in the Austrian courts. It is unthinkable that the manuscript would end up in the hands of the son of the Nazi attorney who appropriated it from my grandfather's estate. But perhaps the more disturbing issue to me and other Austrian Holocaust heirs was revealed in a Gallup poll in 1991. It found that a large portion of Austrians still voiced antisemitism and thought it is time to forget the Holocaust.

But I haven't forgotten what happened, and neither, apparently, has Heiserer. In a legal document he submitted to the Viennese court, he referred to my grandfather as Guido "Israel" Adler and my aunt as Melanie "Sara" Adler. These middle names, like the yellow Star of David on their clothing, were what the Nazis had forced upon the Jews as identifiers and as humiliation. Sixty years after the war, Heiserer continued the practice. I filed a formal complaint about this with the Austrian Bar Association. After several months I received a curt reply. No action would be taken. I thought of the 250,000 Viennese who had gathered in front of the Hofburg in 1938 and wildly cheered as Hitler spoke of the annexation of Austria. The story is not over yet.

Notes

The essential sources referred to in this work are listed below in the notes and as a bibliography separated into primary and secondary sources. The primary sources are mainly made up of unpublished documents, including files from archives in Vienna, Berlin and elsewhere, and letter collections in possession of the Adler family. The secondary sources include books, articles and websites consulted for historical context and insight. The bibliography of secondary sources is not exhaustive; lists of prominent books on Mahler, the Holocaust or World War II would fill volumes of their own.

Notes

1. Synchronicity

"And now I come to the part": Adler, Melanie. Letter to Winifred Wagner, October 26, 1941, Wagner Archives, Bayreuth, Germany.

"Adler's fiftieth birthday": Reilly, Edward. *Gustav Mahler and Guido Adler—Records of a Friendship,* Cambridge, Cambridge University Press, 1982., 103.

"I read with greatest interest"; "The original score": Brosche,
	Gunter. Letter to Tom Adler, Sept.4, 2000; E-mail exchange
	between Tom Adler and Dr. Gunther Brosche of the
	National Library in Vienna, in private possession of the Adler
	family, 2000.
"Because of my father's profession": E-mail Richard Heiserer
	to Tom Adler, September 24, 2000, in private possession of
	the Adler family.

2. Gustav and Guido: The Early Years

Eibenschitz family: Adler, Guido. *Wollen und Wirken: Aus dem
	Leben eines Musikhistorikers*, Wien, Universal Edition, 1935, 2
"Never allow": Ibid., 8
Iglau: City of Jihlava (formerly Iglau) municipal website,
	www.jihlava.cz.
Guido's brothers: Adler, G., *Wollen*, 4
"The best, most gentle": Ibid., 3.
"Later on, she": Ibid., 6.
Vienna background: Brook, Stephen. *Vis á Vis Wien*, Berlin,
	RV Verlag, 1995, 19, 32; *DuMont Visuell Wien*, Köln, DuMont,
	1998, 144.
Conservatory sponsor: Adler, Hubert J., "Guido Adler's Attitude
	towards Religion," Adler family papers, n.d., unpublished,
	in private possession of the Adler family.
"My boy, I like you": Adler, G., *Wollen*, 7.
"Precious relics": Ibid., 8.
"Without hard work": Ibid.
"I was and am": Ibid.
"The youth began being": Ibid., 10.
"I was happy with a Knackwurst": Ibid., 11.
"Overheated fantasy": Ibid., 12.
"You seem to me": Ibid., 13.
"Music dramas and writings": Reilly, 79.
"The bases of harmony": Nettl, Bruno. "The Seminal Eighties:

A North American Perspective of the Beginnings of
Musicology and Ethnomusicology," www2.uji.es/trans/
trans1/nettl.html, 1.
"Is less a matter of artistic": Reilly, 82.
"Really ugly": Adler, Marianne. Conversation with author
(transcribed), November. 22, 1979.

3. The Gift

"Youthfully fresh": Reilly, 84.
"In grateful remembrance": Entry in the Guido Adler
Guestbook by Edward Hanslick, May 9, 1889, Max Berger
Collection, Jewish Museum, Vienna.
"As long as we": Entry in Guido Adler Guestbook by Gustav
Mahler, May 29, 1889.
Czech-German relations/ "German code of honor": Adler,
Hubert J, "Guido Adler and Politics," n.d., unpublished, in
private possession of the Adler family.
"This was my first political": Ibid.
"It was the mark": Engel, Carl. "Guido Adler in Retrospect
(1855-1941)," *The Musical Quarterly,* 1941, p. 392.
"As a priest": Adler, G., *Wollen,* 36.
"My institute": Ibid., 37.
Publishing help: Reilly, 90.
Institute stats: Adler, G., *Wollen,* 37.
"God's blessings": Ibid., 38.
"In many respects": Reilly, 28.
"A little bicycle excursion": Ibid., 95.
"Embrace nature": Ibid., 63.
"When he was suddenly": Keller, James M. "Rückert Lieder,"
New York Philharmonic concert calendar, n.d., *www.
newyorkphilharmonic.org,* 3.
"Ich bin der Welt/ I am lost," lyrics: Rückert, Friedrich. *Ich bin
der Welt abhanden gekommen,* trans. Emily Ezust, www.lieder.net.
"This song, with its": Keller, 3.

The gift: Reilly, 103.

"To my dear friend": Dedication on the manuscript *Ich bin der Welt abhanden gekommen*, trans. Edward Reilly.

"That Adler carefully refrained": Reilly, 103.

"Oh that I were": Mahler, Alma. *Gustav Mahler: Memories and Letters*, trans. Basil Creighton, University of Washington Press, 1968, p. 209.

"It is my very self!": Keller, 3.

"Gustav made a painful": Mahler, 101.

"I have learned that you": Reilly, 108.

"And are we perhaps obligated": Ibid., 111.

Mahler's last years and death: Schreiber, Wolfgang. *Mahler*, Reinbeck bei Hamburg, Rowohlt, 1971, p.124.

"Even before the day": Reilly, 112.

4. 1911 to 1938:Years of Change

WWI views: Adler, Hubert J., "Guido Adler and Religion," n.d., unpublished, in private possession of the Adler family.

Monuments paper: Adler, Hubert J., "Guido Adler on Politics."

Fischmann family: Adler, Marianne. Conversation with author (transcribed), November 22, 1979.

"We embraced, and from": Engel, Carl, 393.

Guido's support for Mahler: Reilly, 114-116 ; Rosenthal, Carl A. "Reminiscences of Guido Adler (1855-1941)," *Musica Judaica*, Journal of the American Society for Jewish Music, Volume VIII, Numer 1, 5747/1985-86, 19.

On Melanie: Auerbach (nee Fischmann), Lisl. Telephone conversations with author, June 15, 2001 and March 2, 2002.

Lannerstrasse: Engel, Carl, 397.

Mahler in Guido's safe: Rosenthal, 19.

Beethoven mask: Inventory of Guido Adler's private library which includes Autograph of Gustav Mahler, undated, in the Guido Adler collection at the University of Georgia, Athens.

5. Decisions

Achim's practice: Adler, Marianne. Conversation with author (transcribed), November 22, 1979.

"It makes me sick": Adler, Hubert J., "Memorandum for Dr. Tischler," (history of the Adlers at the time of the Anschluss), n.d., unpublished, in private possession of the Adler family.

No reinstatement of Guido: Friends of the Music Society of Vienna letter to Guido Adler, October 26, 1939, in private possession of the Adler family.

Engel cable: Adler, Hubert J., "Memorandum for Dr. Tischler."

"We must hereafter call": Engel, Carl, 399.

Referendum: Wiesenthal Museum of Tolerance, www.wiesenthal.com.

"On account of racial problems": Affidavit of Carl Engel for Hamburg-America Line on behalf of Adler family, unpublished, in possession of the Adler family, April 5, 1938

"They promised me": Wiesenthal Museum of Tolerance, op. cit.

Semmering: Auerbach nee Fischmann, Lisl. Telephone conversation with author, June 15, 2001 and March 2, 2002.

Family decision making: Adler, H.J., "Memorandum for Dr. Tischler," op.cit.

Adler family finances: Tax declarations of Guido Adler, Hubert Joachim Adler and Melanie Adler, July 1938, from the Austrian State Archive, Archive of the Republic, Ministry of Finance, Vermögensverkehrsstelle, Vermögensanmeldung (VVSt, VA), 46664 (Guido), 47019 (Melanie), 20208 (Hubert).

"Do you think we could": Adler, Marianne. Conversation with author (transcribed), November 22, 1979.

"The old Adler": Carner, Mosco. "Guido Adler," *The Musical Times*, No. 1142, April 1938, 256.

6. The Vultures Circle

Gestapo at Lannerstrasse : Rosenthal, 20.

"Please don't write anymore": Adler, Melanie. Letter to Hubert J, Adler, October 1938, Adler family letters, unpublished.

Updated taxes: Tax declarations, op. cit.

"The complete nut": Adler, Marianne. Conversation with author (transcribed), November 22, 1979.

"She always took her": Ibid., 18.

"She does certain things": Ibid.

Melanie lesbian theory: Auerbach nee Fischmann, Lisl. Telephone conversation with author, June 15, 2001 and March 2, 2002.

"I wouldn't be surprised": Adler, Marianne. Conversation with author (transcribed), November 22, 1979

"Either you or Marianne": Adler, Guido. Letter to Hubert J. Adler, December 3, 1938, Adler family letters, unpublished.

"Father is healthy but": Adler, Melanie. Letter to Hubert J. Adler, February 27, 1939, Adler family letters, unpublished.

"He's very upset": Ibid.

"I am keeping that secret": Ibid.

"This old man": Adler, Guido. Letter to Hubert J. Adler, April 6, 1939, Adler family letters, unpublished.

Guido's last testament: Enclosed in Adler, Guido. Letter to Hubert J. Adler, May 21, 1939, Adler family letters, unpublished.

Melanie in Munich: Adler, Guido. Letter to Hubert J. Adler, September 28, 1939, Adler family letters, unpublished.

"As you can see from the picture": Adler, Hubert J. Letter to Guido Adler, October 1939, Adler family letters, unpublished.

"Best wishes for your birthday": Adler, Guido. Letter to Evelyn Adler, 1938, Adler family letters, unpublished.

"Yes we live in difficult times": Adler, Guido. Letter to Hubert J. Adler, December 26, 1939, Adler family letters, unpublished.

"They were mostly unemployed": Report of the Claims Conference for Jews in Germany and Austria, Committee for Jewish Claims on Austria, *http://www.claimscon.org/austria/postwar.asp*

Nazi Party leader at Lannerstrasse: Adler, Hubert J., "The Last Years of Guido Adler," n.d., unpublished, in private possession of the Adler family.

"I am living a very secluded life": Adler, Guido. Letter to Hubert J. Adler, November 6, 1940, Adler family letters, unpublished.

Guido's insomnia: Adler, Hubert J., "The Last Years of Guido Adler."

"Slowly, death crept in": Adler, Melanie. Letter to Hubert J. Adler, August 4, 1941, Adler family letters, unpublished.

"I would be very grateful": Leischner, Adolf. Letter to Erich Schenk, January 15, 1941, the Friends of the Music Society of Vienna Archive Library Collections.

"Although it is repugnant": Schenk, Erich. Letter to Adolf Leischner, January 16, 1941, the Friends of the Music Society of Vienna Archive Library Collections.

"I have taken steps": Wagner, Winifred. Letter to Melanie Adler, January 17, 1941, Guido Adler Guestbook, Max Berger Collection, Jewish Museum, Vienna.

"Utter incoherent sentences": Adler, Hubert J., "The Last Years of Guido Adler."

"Then he became bedridden": Adler, Melanie. Letter to Hubert J. Adler, August 4, 1941. "Deep unconsciousness": Ibid.

7. Emerging Self-Interests

Adler family attorneys: Adler family probate records, District Court Döbling, Vienna, Files: 5 A 426/47; 1 A 214/41.

Walter Redlich: Ibid., declaration of January 14, 1940.

"The profession of lawyer": Luebke, David M. "Principal Acts of Anti-Jewish Legislation in Germany, 1933-1942," University of Oregon, *http://www.uoregon.edu/~dluebke/NaziGermany410/Judenpolitik.html*

Heiserer's Nazi background: File on Richard Heiserer, Austrian
    Federal Ministry of the Interior, Vienna, Dept. 2. From the
    Gau [party district] document nr. 56226.

"His conduct toward the party": Ibid.

"In the fiscal and economic interest": Heiserer, Richard. Letter
    to Gaurecthsamt of the N.S.D.A.P., Vienna, September 11,
    1939, Ibid.

Heiserer regrets loss of 80,000: Ibid.

"According to our laws legally": Walzer, Tina and Templ,
    Stephan. *Unser Wien: Arisierung auf Österreich*, Berlin: Aufbau-
    Verlag, 2001, 38.

"I calmly accepted my lack": Ficker, Rudolf von. Letter to Egon
    Wellesz, January 29, 1947, Ficker-Wellesz letters, 1946-1948,
    found in the Austrian National Library Music Collection,
    Wellesz Memorial Collection, Vienna.

"Hardly had everything been resolved": Adler, Melanie. Letter
    to Erich Schenk, written between February 15 and March
    10, 1941, the Friends of the Music Society of Vienna Archive
    Library Collections.

Schenk's offer: Ficker, Rudolf von. Letter to Egon Wellesz,
    September 1, 1947.

"I told her that at least": Ibid.

Schenk background, Austrian Ministry of Education, Science
    and Culture, www.aeiou.at.

"Schenk's ardent Nazi sympathies": Letter by Egon Wellesz,
    n.d., in Ficker-Wellesz letter collection.

"Extremely negative assessment": Central Office of the Cultural
    Politics Archive letter to the director of the NSDAP district
    of Rostock City, December 3, 1937, Bundesarchiv Berlin,
    NS/15 132 B. 48.

"Our own experiences have mainly shown": Ibid.

Schenk book review: *The Strauß Dynasty*, review by Erich Schenk,
    November 23, 1939, in DBFUA file, Bundesarchiv Berlin-
    Lichterfelde. Arch. NS/15 101 fol. 1-149, place 51, house
    904, Bl. 115 A/B

"It is likely that Schenk": Potter, Pamela. *Most German of the rts.*

Musicology and Society from the Weimar Republic to the End of Hitler's Reich, New Haven: Yale University Press, 1998, 108.
"I as representative of the German": "Ahnenerbe" file of Prof. Dr. phil. Erich Schenk, 05.05.02, Berlin Document Center, in Bundesarchiv Berlin-Lichterfelde.
"Always proudly wore the party badge": Ficker, Rudolf von. Letter to Egon Wellesz, July 2, 1946.
"A few weeks ago, the founder": Schenk, Erich. Letter to Ministerialrat Frey, Reichs Ministry of Education, Vienna, March 31, 1941, found in Bundesarchiv-Lichterfelde, ZstA REM 2176 Bl. 13-16.
"Since the library consisted nearly": Ficker, Rudolf von. Memorandum to Staatskommissariat für alle unmittelbaren Bundesangelegenheiten im Lande Tirol, October 29, 1945, as copied in the archive of the University of Innsbruck.
Zuth library purchase: Schenk, Erich. Letter to Ministerialrat Frey, Reichs Ministry of Education, Vienna, December 18, 1942, found in Bundesarchiv-Lichterfelde, file "Reichs Ministry for Science, Education, and Instruction of the Public—re: University of Vienna, Music Science Seminar—July 1940 to January 1944," Bl. 22.
"They not only offered Ms. Adler": Ficker, Rudolf von. Letter to Otto (Baron von) Skrbensky, February 25, 1946, Ficker-Wellesz letter collection.

8. The Betrayal

"Meetings with professors Haas and Nowak": Heiserer, Richard. Letter to Erich Schenk, April 4, 1941, the Friends of the Music Society of Vienna Archive Library Collections.
"To Dr. Heiserer, Attorney, Vienna I, Opernring": Ficker, Rudolf von. Letter to Richard Heiserer, April 9, 1941, in Melanie Adler-Rudolf von Ficker letters, Austrian National Library Music Collection, the Wellesz Memorial Collection.
"My letter may hardly be in your hands": Adler, Melanie. Letter to Rudolf von Ficker, May 4, 1941, Ibid.

"This circumstance, though seemingly a trifle": Adler, Melanie. Letter to Rudolf von Ficker, May 6, 1941, Ibid.

"What is the true intention" and responses: Ibid.

"I already wrote to you that this man": Ibid.

Heiserer assigned to probate: District Court Döbling, Vienna, File: 1 A 214/41.

Melanie's right to inherit: Ibid., declaration of May 27, 1941.

"The City library has contacted the attorney": Adler, Melanie. Letter to Rudolf von Ficker, late May 1941, Melanie Adler-Rudolf von Ficker letters.

Borufka appraisal: Hamann, Brigitte. "Der Welt abhanden gekommen? Guido Adler und die Musik," *Das Jüdische Echo*, vol. 49, October 2000, 329-331.

"But this was still done under Dr. H": Adler, Melanie. Letter to Rudolf von Ficker, June 1941, Melanie Adler-Rudolph von Ficker letters.

"In reference to my telephone conversation": Heiserer, Richard. Letter to the Music Science Seminar, Vienna, June 27, 1941. The Friends of Music Society of Vienna Archive Library Collections.

Schenk's response to Heiserer: Schenk, Erich. Letter to Richard Heiserer, June 28, 1941. The Friends of the Music Society of Vienna Archive Library Collections.

"Thus from the very beginning": Ficker, Rudolf von. Letter to Otto (Baron von) Skrbensky, February 25, 1946, Ficker-Wellesz letter collection.

"About ten days ago I changed attorneys": Adler, Melanie. Letter to Rudolf von Ficker, June 1941, Melanie Adler—Rudolf von Ficker letters.

"I haven't had an hour's peace": Adler, Melanie. Letter to Rudolf von Ficker, July 7, 1941, Ibid.

"After every library visit, Dr. Heiserer": Ficker, Rudolf von. Letter to Egon Wellesz, September 1, 1947.

"Suspected that the attorney Dr. Heiserer's hostile": Ibid.

"Some attorneys, including Dr. Heiserer": Report: "re: Dr. Melanie Adler, Confiscation of Assets," by Türk, official of the Regional Tax Authority Office, Vienna, June 7, 1945,

Adler family probate records, District Court Döbling, Vienna, File: 5 A 426/47.

"Legal situation was somewhat muddled": Ibid.

"Complicity was of high importance": Waltzer and Templ, 38.

"Corruption and greed": Ibid.

"Two days ago the attorney spent": Adler, Melanie. Letter to Rudolf von Ficker, August 6, 1941.

"We are interested in literature": copied in Adler, Melanie. Letter to Rudolf von Ficker, August 8, 1941.

"Munich didn't make any offer at all": Ficker, Rudolf von. Letter to Egon Wellesz, September 1, 1947.

9. The Last Hope

Background, Winifred Wagner: Hamann, Brigitte. *Winifred Wagner oder Hitlers Bayreuth*, München: Piper Verlag, 2002.

"Pull the sword out of the German oak": Umbach, Klaus. "Das herrscherliche Wurzelweib," *Der Spiegel* 21/2002, 67.

"Where I can prevent an act of violence": Ibid., 168.

Winifred helps others: Hamann, *Winifred Wagner* 450

"It's high time that something has to happen": Adler, Melanie. Letter to Rudolf von Ficker, July 7, 1941, Melanie Adler— Rudolf von Ficker letters, Austrian National Library Music Collection, the Wellesz Memorial Collection.

"From these three gentlemen": Ficker, Rudolf von. Letter to B. Wetzelsberger, July 21, 1941, in Melanie Adler-Rudolf von Ficker letters, Ibid.

"Unfortunately, your letter was forwarded": Wagner, Winifred. Letter to Melanie Adler, copied in Melanie Adler letter to Ficker, August 24, 1941, Ibid.

"I have come to the opinion": Adler, Melanie. Letter to Rudolf von Ficker, September 15, 1941, Ibid.

"All of the personal property": Adler family probate records, District Court Döbling, declaration of September 26, 1941.

"The deportations to Poland begin again": Adler, Melanie. Letter to Rudolf von Ficker, Saturday, October 1941, Melanie Adler-Rudolf von Ficker letters.

"I now know definitely that Professor": Ibid.

"Most revered, merciful lady": Adler, Melanie. Letter to Winifred Wagner, October 26, 1941, from the Wagner Archives, Bayreuth.

"This is what it is like now": Adler, Melanie. Letter to Rudolf von Ficker, November 11, 1941, Melanie Adler-Rudolf von Ficker letters.

"I have thought over again and again": Wagner, Winifred. Letter to Melanie Adler, copied in Melanie Adler letter to Ficker, November 11, 1941, Melanie Adler-Rudolf von Ficker letters.

"Lived in hiding": Testimony of Karola Fischmann, Landesgericht für Zivilrechtssachen Wien No. 48 T 2027/46.

"I was received most warmly": Adler, Melanie. Letter to Rudolf von Ficker, December 14, 1941, Melanie Adler-Rudolf von Ficker letters.

"Had taken the matter of protection": Hamann, *Winifred Wagner*, 455.

"In the meantime, I have turned personally" Adler, Melanie. Letter to Rudolf von Ficker, December 1941, Melanie Adler-Rudolf von Ficker letters.

"Of course, this plan could not be carried out": Winifred Wagner Denkschrift, eingereicht von der Verteidigung bei der Spruchkammer Bayreuth. Spruchkammerakt Winifred Wagner 1894, Staatsarchiv München, n.d., 36.

"Had no choice but to let the Gestapo": Ficker, Rudolf von. Letter to Otto (Baron von) Skrbensky, February 25, 1946, Ficker-Wellesz letter collection.

"Prof. Schenk had called this behavior": Ibid.

Melanie's fate: Amtsblatt and Deportationsliste, Dokumentationsarchiv des österreichischen Widerstandes (DÖW).

"For the transport of the sick": Moser J. *Die Judenverfolgung in Österreich 1938-1945*, Vienna, 1966.

"In order to get the Aktion": Letter from Dr. Becker to SS-

Obersturmbahnführer Rauff, May 16, 1942 in "Extermination in Gas Vans in the Ukraine, 1942." Yad-Vashem Holocaust Documents, 2002. www.yad-vashem.org.il/about_holocaust/documents/part3/doc191.html

10. Ficker's Mission

Background, post-war Austria: Wistrich, Robert. "Austria and the Legacy of the Holocaust," booklet for the American Jewish Committee, New York, 1999; *Österreich im 20. Jahrhundert*, Wien/Köln/Weimar: Böhlau-Studien-Bücher, 1997; "Kriegsende und Nachkriegszeit," Bundesministerium für Bildung, Wissenschaft und Kultur, *http://www.aeiou.at/aeiou.history.gtour.krieg*; Bailer, Brigitte, "Der 'antifaschistische Geist' der Nachkriegszeit," lecture delivered at a symposium at the University of Paris, December 1999, found at *http://www.doew.at/thema/antifageist/antifageist.html* etc.

"Austria is reminded": "Austria's International Legal Status between 1938 and 1945 and Austrian Restitution Efforts," publication of the Austrian Government, *www.austria nembassy.ee/erestitut.html*, 2002, 2.

"No reparation shall be extracted": Ibid., 4

"Thus, the burden of proof": Ibid., 6.

"It was not easy": Wistrich, 15.

"Austrian officials quietly": Chesnoff, Richard Z. *Pack of Thieves: How Hitler and Europe Plundered the Jews and Committed the Greatest Theft in History*, New York: Doubleday, 1999, 40.

Small amount returned: Claims Conference for Jews in Germany and Austria, reports on compensation and restitution: *http://www.claimscon.org/gsf/history.asp*

"Jewish character was": Wistrich, 8.

"Something had to be done": Ibid.

"There is no institute": Ficker, Rudolf von. Letter to Egon Wellesz, December 24, 1946, Ficker-Wellesz letters 1946-1948, found in the Austrian National Library Music Collection, Wellesz Memorial Collection.

"Honest desire to return": Ibid.

"In hindsight on the friendly": Ficker, Rudolf von. Memo to Staatskommission, October 29, 1945.

Orel fired: Potter 108

"The best Austrian scholars": Fleck, Christian. "The Restoration of Austrian Universities after World War II". For the Center for Austrian Studies, July 1995, 3.

"The main techniques used to retain": Ibid., 4.

"My closest colleague": Ficker, Rudolf von. Letter to Egon Wellesz, April 21, 1946.

"At that time in the university": Goller, Peter and Oberkofler, Gerhard. "Krise der Wissenschaftspolitik und Faschismus an österreichs Universitäten," *Jahrbuch 1996*, Dokumentationsarchiv des österreichischen Widerstandes, Vienna, 120.

"Prof. Schenk and his representatives": Ficker, Rudolf von. Letter to Otto (Baron von) Skrbensky, February 25, 1946, Ficker-Wellesz letter collection.

"In contrast, Prof. Schenk has": Ibid.

"for his merits": Ficker,Rudolf von. Letter to Egon Wellesz, June 6, 1946.

"Schenk had stated that all": Ficker, Rudolf von. Letter to Egon Wellesz, July 8, 1946.

"When Ms. Adler refused": Ficker, Rudolf von. Letter to Otto (Baron von) Skrbensky, July 2, 1946, Ficker-Wellesz letter collection.

11. Voices in the Dark

"Naturally, I was very worried": Ficker, Rudolf von. Letter to Wellesz, October 30, 1946, Ficker-Wellesz letters 1946-1948, found in the Austrian National Library Music Collection, Wellesz Memorial Collection.

"A threat to intimidate": Ficker, Rudolf von. Letter to Egon Wellesz, September 23, 1946.

Ficker's career: Staatskommissariat cover to Ficker's memo, October 29, 1945.

"Not politically flawless": Ibid.

Ficker forced to return to Munich: Ficker, Rudolf von. Letter to Egon Wellesz, October 30, 1946.

"I was to be deported": Ficker, Rudolf von. Letter to Egon Wellesz, January 29, 1947.

"The accusations against": Hayek, Friedrich. Letter to Fritz Saxl, October 17, 1946, found in Ficker-Wellesz letter collection.

"Is annulled by the letters": Wellesz, Egon. Letter to Fritz Saxl, October 22, 1946, found in Ficker-Wellesz letter collection

"Vague accusations of all kinds": Hayek, Friedrich. Letter to Fritz Saxl, October 17, 1946, Ficker-Wellesz letter collection.

"Hayek gets his information": Ficker, Rudolf von. Letter to Egon Wellesz, October 30, 1946.

"The persons nominated," etc.: Skrbensky, Otto (Baron von). Letter to Friedrich Hayek, with Hayek's handwritten comments in the margins, December 4, 1946, found in Ficker-Wellesz letter collection.

Melanie declared dead: Landesgericht for ZRS, File: 48 T 2027/46, January 28, 1947.

"The Schenk affair seems": Ficker, Rudolf von. Letter to Egon Wellesz, May 6, 1947.

"About Achim A.": Ibid.

State of Adler property and library: Report: "re: Dr. Melanie Adler, Confiscation of

Assets," June 7, 1945.

"But it is surprising": Ibid.

Schenk's inventory: Tax Authority Office of Vienna letter to attorney Hans Wiala, n.d., refers to a letter from Erich Schenk to Tax Authority from July 30, 1947, Adler family probate records, File: ZI.XIII-4074-1/47, Sub file: AZ 05205-P6b-6.

Some material returned to Wiala: Ibid.

Wiala's inventory: Ibid.

"Private correspondence": Erich Schenk letter to the Tax Authority Office of Vienna, September 8, 1947, Adler family probate records.

Portion of the library to Georgia: Reilly, Edward. *The Papers of Guido Adler at the University of Georgia: A Provisional Inventory*, n.p., 1975.

"Universally respected": Wellesz, Egon. Unaddressed, undated letter found in Ficker-Wellesz letter collection

Heiserer's denazification: File on Heiserer, Austrian Federal Ministry of the Interior, op. cit.

12. The Reckoning

"This sent a clear signal": from "Schlechtes Zeugnis für Österreich." MEZ, 5 July 2002.

"Comprehensive compensation for": Austrian Information Service press releases: "Austria Prepares Restitution of Art Stolen by Nazis", Washington, D.C., September 9, 1998, also from December 16, 1998, and January 19, 2001.

Background restitution: "Survey of Past Austrian Measures of Restitution, Compensation and Social Welfare for Victims of National Socialism." Office of the Special Envoy for Restitution Issues Ernst Sucharipa, October 2000.

"The Klimts were taken": Lubkin, Martha. "Austria may be sued in the U.S. in claim hat it forced Jew to give Klimts after World War II: Austria is not an adequate forum to resolve Nazi loot claim says California federal court," *The Art Newspaper*, August 18, 2001.

Schnitzler manuscript and Sotheby's: E-mail exchange between Tom Adler and Sotheby's Auction House attorney Jonathan Olsoff, 2000, in private possession of the Adler family.

"Let me begin by assuring you": Jonathan Olsoff e-mail to Tom Adler, December 6, 2000, Ibid.

Gallup poll 1991: Wistrich, 25.

Heiserer's filing with Nazi names: Lawsuit Tom Adler v. Richard Heiserer, Landesgericht für ZRS Wien No GZ: 27 Cg 191/01y.

Bibliography

Primary sources

Adler family letters, unpublished, in private possession of the author.

Adler family probate records, District Court Döbling, Vienna, Files: 5 A 426/47 (Melanie Adler); 1 A 214/41 (Guido Adler).

Adler, Hubert J. "Guido Adler's Attitude towards Religion," n.d., in private possession of the Adler family.

—"Guido Adler and Politics," n.d., unpublished, in private possession of the Adler family.

—"The Last Years of Guido Adler (1938-1941)," n.d., unpublished, in private possession of the Adler family.

—"Memorandum for Dr. Tischler," (history of the Adlers at the time of the Anschluss), n.d., unpublished, in private possession of the Adler family.

Adler, Marianne. Conversation with author (transcribed), November 22, 1979, unpublished, in private possession of the Adler family.

Adler, Melanie. Letter to Erich Schenk, written between February 15 and March 10, 1941, The Friends of Music Society of Vienna Archive Library Collections.

Adler, Melanie. Letters to Rudolf von Ficker, 1941, Austrian National Library Music Collection, the Wellesz Memorial Collection.

Adler, Melanie. Letter to Winifred Wagner, October 26, 1941 Wagner Archives, Bayreuth, Germany.

Affidavit of Carl Engel for Hamburg-America Line on behal of Adler family, in private possession of the Adler family April 5,1938.

"Ahnenerbe" file of Prof. Dr. phil. Erich Schenk, 05.05.02 Berlin Document Center, in Bundesarchiv, Berlin Lichterfelde.

Auerbach neé Fischmann, Lisl. Telephone conversations with author, June 15, 2001 and March 2, 2002.

Central Office of the Cultural Politics Archive letter to the director of the NSDAP district of Rostock City regarding Erich Schenk, 3 Dec. 1937, Bundesarchiv Berlin, NS/1 132 B. 48.

Declaration of death, Melanie Adler, Landesgericht for ZRS Vienna, File: 48 T 2027/46.

Deportation of Melanie Adler, Amtsblatt and Deportationsliste Dokumentationsarchiv des österreichischen Widerstande (DÖW).

E-mail exchange between Tom Adler and Dr. Gunther Brosch of the National Library in Vienna, in private possession of the Adler family, 2000.

E-mail exchange between Tom Adler and Sotheby's Auction House attorney Jonathan Olsoff, in private possession of the Adler family, 2000.

Ficker, Rudolf von. Letter to Richard Heiserer, April 9, 194 the Austrian National Library Music Collection, the Welles Memorial Collection.

Ficker, Rudolf von. Memorandum to Staatskommissariat f alle unmittelbaren Bundesangelegenheiten im Lan

Tirol, October 29, 1945, as copied in the archive of the University of Innsbruck.

Ficker (Rudolf von)-Wellesz (Egon) letters 1946-1948, the Austrian National Library Music Collection, the Wellesz Memorial Collection.

File on Richard Heiserer, Austrian Federal Ministry of the Interior, Vienna, Dept. 2,—From the Gau [party district] document nr. 56226.

Friends of the Music Society of Vienna letter to Guido Adler, October 26, 1939, in private possession of the Adler family.

Guido Adler Guestbook, Max Berger Collection, Jewish Museum, Vienna.

Heiserer, Richard. E-mail to Tom Adler, September 24, 2000, in private possession of the Adler family.

Heiserer, Richard. Letter to Erich Schenk, April 4, 1941. The Friends of Music Society of Vienna Archive Library Collections.

Heiserer, Richard. Letter to Gaurecthsamt der N.S.D.A.P., Vienna, 11 September 1939. Records of Austrian Ministry of Interior Affairs.

Heiserer, Richard. Letter to Music Science Seminar, Vienna, June 27, 1941. The Friends of Music Society of Vienna Archive Library Collections.

Inventory of Guido Adler's private library which includes autograph Gustav Mahler, undated, in the Guido Adler collection at the University of Georgia, Athens.

Lawsuit Tom Adler v. Richard Heiserer, Landesgericht für ZRS Wien No GZ: 27 Cg 191/01y.

Leischner, Adolf. Letter to Erich Schenk, letter asking for Guido Adler's world reputation, 15 January, 1941. The Friends of Music Society of Vienna Archive Library Collections.

Report: "re: Dr. Melanie Adler, Confiscation of Assets," by Türk, official of the Regional Tax Authority Office, Vienna, June 7, 1945, Adler probate records, District Court Döbling, Vienna.

Röckel, Karl-Alexander. "Report on Interrogation and Examination of Correspondence of Mrs. Winnifred Wagner [*sic*]," Hardheim, March 27, 1947. Headquarters CIC Detachment 970/65 APO 102, U.S. Army. Staatsarchiv München, Spruchkammerakt Winifred Wagner 1894.

Schenk, Erich. Letter to Adolf Leischner, 16 January, 1941. The Friends of Music Society of Vienna Archive Library Collections.

Schenk, Erich. Letter to Ministerialrat Frey, Reichs Ministry of Education, Vienna, March 31, 1941, found in Bundesarchiv Berlin-Lichterfelde, ZstA REM 2176 Bl. 13-16.

Schenk, Erich. Letter to Ministerialrat Frey, Reichs Ministry of Education, Vienna, December 18, 1942, found in Bundesarchiv, Berlin-Lichterfelde, file labeled Reich Ministry for Science, Education and the Instruction of the Public-University of Vienna, Musicological Seminar—Jul 1940 to January 1944.

The Strauß Dynasty, review by Erich Schenk, November 23, 1939 in DBFUA file, Bundesarchiv, Berlin-Lichterfelde. Arch NS/15 101 fol. 1-149, place 51, house 904, Bl. 115 A/B.

Tax declarations of Guido Adler, Hubert Joachim Adler and Melanie Adler, July 1938, from the Austrian State Archive, Archive of the Republic, Ministry of Finance, Vermögensverkehrsstelle, Vermögensanmeldung (VVS VA), 46664 (Guido), 47019 (Melanie), 20208 (Hubert)

Tax Authority Office of Vienna letter to attorney Hans Wial n.d., refers to a letter from Erich Schenk to Tax Authority from, July 30, 1947, Adler family probate records, District Court Döbling, File ZI.XIII-4074-1/47, Sub file: AZ 0520 P6b-6.

Testimony of Karola Fischmann, Landesgericht für Zivilrechtssachen Wien No. 48 T 2027/46

Wagner, Winifred. Letter to Melanie Adler, January 17, 194 Guido Adler Guestbook, Max Berger Collection, Jewi Museum, Vienna.

Winifred Wagner Denkschrift, eingereicht von der Verteidigu bei der Spruchkammer Bayreuth. Spruchkammera Winifred Wagner 1894, Staatsarchiv München. n.d.

Secondary Sources

Adler, Guido. *Gustav Mahler*, published in English in *Gustav Mahler and Guido Adler* by Edward Reilly, Cambridge, Cambridge University Press, 1982.

—*Wollen und Wirken: Aus dem Leben eines Musikhistorikers*, Wien, Universal Edition, 1935.

Austrian Information Service press release: "Austria Prepares Restitution of Art Stolen by Nazis," Washington, D.C., September 9, 1998.

—on restitution, December 16, 1998.

—January 19, 2001.

"Austria's Burden of History," News in Review, CBC report, April 2000. //cbc.ca/newsinreview/April%202000/ Haider/burden2.html

"Austria's International Legal Status between 1938 and 1945 and Austrian Restitution Efforts," Austrian Government publication, *www.austrianembassy.ee/erestitut.html*, 2002.

Bailer, Brigitte, "Der 'antifaschistische Geist' der Nachkriegszeit," lecture delivered at a symposium at the University of Paris, December 1999, found at *http:// www.doew.at/thema/antifageist/antifageist.html*

Beller, Steven. *Vienna and the Jews*, Cambridge, Cambridge University Press, 1989.

Brief biography of Carl Engel, www.altenberg.co.at/txt/ blo24_e.htm.

Brook, Stephen. *Vis á Vis Wien*, Berlin, RV Verlag, 1995.

Bukey, Evan Burr. *Hitlers Österreich. 'Eine Bewegung und ein Volk'*, Munich: Europa Verlag, 2001.

Carner, Mosco. "Guido Adler," *The Musical Times*, No. 1142, April 1938

—and Eder, Gabriele, "Guido Adler," *www.grovemusic.com*

Chesnoff, Richard Z. *Pack of Thieves: How Hitler and Europe Plundered the Jews and Committed the Greatest Theft in History*, New York: Doubleday, 1999.

City of Jihlava (formerly Iglau) municipal website, *www.jihlava.cz.*

Claims Conference for Jews in Germany and Austria,

Committee for Jewish Claims on Austria report on postwar Austria, *http://www.claimscon.org/austria/postwar.asp*

Czeike, Felix. *Historisches Lexikon Wien*, Wien: Kremayr & Scheriau, 1992-1997.

"Deportationen in das 'Reichskommissariat Ostland', 1941/42, Maly Trostinec." Dokumentationsarchiv des österreichschen Widerstandes.

DuMont Visuell Wien, Köln, DuMont, 1998.

Encyclopedia of the Holocaust, New York, Macmillan Publishing, 1990.

Engel, Carl. "Guido Adler in Retrospect (1855-1941)," *The Musical Quarterly,*1941, 391.

Engel, Gabriel. Gustav Mahler—Song Symphonist, Bruckner Society of America, 1932.

Enigl, Marianne. "Abhanden gekommen," *profil* magazine, Vienna, October 16, 2000,. 42.

"Extermination in Gas Vans in the Ukraine, 1942." Yad-Vashem Holocaust Documents, 2002. www.yad-vashem.org.il/about_holocaust/documents/part3/doc191.html.

Fleck, Christian. "The Restoration of Austrian Universities after World War II." For the Center for Austrian Studies, July 1995.

Geburtstag von Erich Schenk, Stadt Wien: www.wien.gv.at/ma53/45jahre/1962/0562.htm

Gilbert, Martin. *Endlösung: Die Vertreibung und Vernichtung der Juden, Ein Atlas*. Reinbeck bei Hamburg, Rowohlt Verlag, 1982.

Goller, Peter and Oberkofler, Gerhard. "Krise der Wissenschaftspolitik und Faschismus an österreichs Universitäten," *Jahrbuch 1996*, Dokumentationsarchiv des österreichischen Widerstandes, Vienna, 101-122.

Grange, Henry Louis de la. *Gustav Mahler: Vienna, Triumph and Disillusion (1904-1907)*, vol. 3 of Gustav Mahler series, Oxford: Oxford University Press, 2000.

"Gustav Mahler (1860-1911)," BBC Music Profiles, *www.bbc.co.uk/music/profiles/print/mahler.shtml*.

Hamann, Brigitte. "Der Welt abhanden gekommen? Guido

Adler und die Musik," *Das Jüdische Echo*, vol. 49, Oct 2000, 329-331

—*Winifred Wagner oder Hitlers Bayreuth*, München: Piper Verlag, 2002.

Ingalls, Zoe. "The Works of a Founding Father of Modern Musicology," *The Chronicle of Higher Education*, March 3, 1995.

Keller, James M. "Rückert Lieder," New York Philharmonic concert calendar, www.newyorkphilharmonic.org, n.d.

"Kriegsende und Nachkriegszeit," Bundesministerium für Bildung, Wissenschaft und Kultur, *http://www.aeiou.at/aeiou.history.gtour.krieg*

Luebke, David M. "Principal Acts of Anti-Jewish Legislation in Germany, 1933-1942," University of Oregon, *http://www.uoregon.edu/~dluebke/NaziGermany410/Judenpolitik.html*.

Lufkin, Martha. "Austria says it is immune from lawsuits in U.S. over alleged Nazi-looted Klimts: But can publication of catalogue by Yale Press in U.S. subject it to lawsuit here?" *The Art newspaper*, 2002.

—"Austria may be sued in the U.S. in claim that it forced Jew to give Klimts after World War II: Austria is not an adequate forum to resolve Nazi loot claim says California federal court," *The Art Newspaper*, August 18, 2001.

Mahler, Alma. *Gustav Mahler: Memories and Letters*, trans. Basil Creighton, University of Washington Press, 1968.

Mauthausen Concentration Camp website, *www.mauthausen-memorial.gv.at/engl/Aktuell/presse-e.htm*

Moser J. *Die Judenverfolgung in Österreich 1938-1945*, Vienna, 1966.

Nettl, Bruno. "The Seminal Eighties: A North American Perspective of the Beginnings of Musicology and Ethnomusicology," www2.uji.es/trans/trans1/nettl.html.

Neuffer, Elizabeth and Robinson, Walter V. "Austria confronts dark past by combing art for Nazi links," *Boston Globe*, March 5, 1998.

Oberkofler, Gerhard. "Orchideen Fächer im Faschismus," *Jahrbuch 1990*, Dokumentationsarchiv des österreichischen Widerstandes, 45.

Österreich im 20. Jahrhundert, Wien/Köln/Weimar: Böhlau-
Studien-Bücher, 1997.

Potter, Pamela. *Most German of the Arts: Musicology and Society
from the Weimar Republic to the End of Hitler's Reich*, New Haven:
Yale University Press, 1998.

Reilly, Edward. *Gustav Mahler and Guido Adler—Records of a
Friendship*, Cambridge, Cambridge University Press, 1982.

—*The Papers of Guido Adler at the University of Georgia: A Provisional
Inventory*, n.p., 1975.

Remarks by Ambassador Ernst Sucharipa on the Occassion of a
Press Conference on 17 January 2001: Regarding the
Signing of a Holocaust Compensation Agreement (in
Austria). http://www.austria.org/press/237.html

"Restitution of Stolen Property," report of Radio Österreich
International, http://roi.orf.at/english/kultur/
restitution.html

Revers, Peter. *Mahlers Lieder: Eine musikalischer Werkführe*
Munich: Beck, 2000.

Rosenthal, Carl A. "Reminiscences of Guido Adler (185?-
1941)," *Musica Judaica*, Journal of the American Society
for Jewish Music, Volume VIII, Numer 1, 5747/1985-86.

Rückert, Friedrich. *Ich bin der Welt abhanden gekommen*, tran
Emily Ezust, www.lieder.net.

"Schlechtes Zeugnis für Österreich." MEZ, 5 July 2002.

Schreiber, Wolfgang. *Mahler*, Reinbeck bei Hamburg: Rowohl
1971.

Spotts, Frederic. *Bayreuth, A History of the Wagner Festival.* Ne
Haven and London: Yale University Press, 1994.

"Survey of Past Austrian Measures of Restitution, Compensatic
and Social Welfare for Victims of National Socialism." Offi
of the Special Envoy for Restitution Issues Ernst Sucharip
October 2000.

Twain, Mark. "Stirring Times in Austria," *Harper's New Montl
Magazine*, March 1898.

Umbach, Klaus. "Das herrscherliche Wurzelweib," *Der Spie*
21/2002, 166-170

Wagner, Richard. "Judaism in Music," trans. William Ashton Ellis, *Richard Wagner's Prose Works Volume III*, 1894.

Walzer, Tina and Templ, Stephan. *Unser Wien: Arisierung auf Österreich*, Berlin: Aufbau-Verlag, 2001.

Wank, Solomon. "The Nationalities Question in the Habsburg Monarchy: Reflections on the Historical Record," Franklin & Marshall College, Working Paper for the Center for Austrian Studies, April 1993.

Wasinger, Andrea. "Streit um Gustav Mahlers Lied," *Kurier*, Vienna, January 21, 2001.

Who's Who in Nazi Germany. London: Wiederfield and Nicolsa, 1982.

Wiedemann, Erich. "Die Kunsträuber," *Der Spiegel*, 25/2001.

Wiesenthal Museum of Tolerance, www.wiesenthal.com.

Wimmer, Adi. "The Lesser Traumatized: Exile Narratives of Austrian Jews," working paper, University of Klagenfurt, 1999.

Wistrich, Robert. "Austria and the Legacy of the Holocaust," booklet for the American Jewish Committee, New York, 1999.

Made in the USA
Lexington, KY
19 February 2012